YORK NOTES

General Editors: Professor A.N.Jeffares (*University of Stirling*) & Professor Suheil Bushrui (*American University*)

CW01096068

Alaı

CRY, THE BELOVED COUNTRY

Notes by Geoffrey M. Ridden

BA M PHIL (LEEDS)
Principal Lecturer in English,
King Alfred's College, Winchester

LONGMAN
YORK PRESS

Extracts from *Cry, the Beloved Country* by Alan Paton are reprinted by kind permission of the author and Jonathan Cape Ltd, London; and in the U.S.A. by kind permission of Charles Scribner's Sons, copyright 1948, 1976 Alan Paton. (New York: Charles Scribner's Sons, 1948)

YORK PRESS
Immeuble Esseily, Place Riad Solh, Beirut.

LONGMAN GROUP LIMITED
Longman House,
Burnt Mill,
Harlow,
Essex

First published 1983
Second impression 1984
ISBN 0 582 79217 7

Printed in Hong Kong by
Sheck Wah Tong Printing Press Ltd

Contents

Part 1

Introduction

Alan Paton

Alan Stewart Paton was born on 11 January 1903 in Pietermaritzburg in Natal, which was at that time a British Colony in Southern Africa. His father was a civil servant who had been born in Scotland; his mother, a former teacher, had spent all her life in Natal. He was educated at Maritzburg College and at Natal University College before embarking on a career as a teacher. After eleven years in this profession he left to take charge of the Diepkloof Reformatory for delinquent African boys, near Johannesburg. His experiences there are reflected in the description of reformatory life in *Cry, the Beloved Country* and, more specifically, in his short stories.

Whilst at Diepkloof, Paton's writing changed from the poetry which he had written and published as a student to the field of political non-fiction. He was passionately interested in the question of the social conditions in his country, and on the effects of these conditions on crime, especially by young offenders. In 1946 he took leave of absence from Diepkloof and travelled extensively to study penal institutions throughout Europe and North America, learning not only about the treatment of crime in these various countries but also the different ways in which they had fared as a result of the Second World War. During this journey, while he was able to look with more detachment at South Africa, Paton began to write *Cry, the Beloved Country*, which was so successful on its publication in 1948 that he resigned his post at Diepkloof to devote himself to writing. The year 1948 was also a turning-point in the politics of South Africa, for it saw the victory of the Nationalist Malan administration which introduced the policy of separate racial development known as *apartheid*. Paton has always been fundamentally opposed to this policy and his opposition is clearly manifest in his fictional and non-fictional writing.

In December 1948 Jan Hofmeyr, a great liberal South African politician, friend of Paton and political opponent of Malan, died, and Paton began to work on his biography, living at the time with Hofmeyr's mother. Although the work did not go smoothly because of disputes with Mrs Hofmeyr, Paton was able to demonstrate his commitment to the man in a different way by becoming a founder member of the Liberal Party of South Africa, formed in 1953, and its president from 1958 until the party was finally made illegal in 1968.

Paton has continued to campaign in print against *apartheid*, his own political insight developing in ways which have led him to be critical of the methods employed by his own Liberal Party and to recognise the reasons why the Party failed to realise its aims. He finally published his biography of Hofmeyr* in 1964 and that work, together with his biography of Archbishop Clayton, published in 1973, demonstrate his conviction that racism and Christianity are totally incompatible. There were those who felt that Paton's political activities had completely eclipsed his writing of fiction for, after the publication in 1953 of his second novel, *Too Late the Phalarope*, and of a volume of short stories in 1961 (published under the title *Tales from a Troubled Land* in the USA and as *Debbie Go Home* in Great Britain), there was a long silence broken only by his biographies, his political prose, and some writing for the non-racial theatre. Paton has, however, at last published his long-awaited third novel, *Ah, But Your Land is Beautiful* (1981) and we are promised a second volume of autobiography to complete the work begun in his first, *Towards the Mountain* (1980).

Alan Paton married his first wife Doris Francis in 1928, and they had two children. After her death in 1967 he married Anne Hopkins in 1969. He remains one of the the most significant and influential figures in South Africa, whose voice is so respected internationally that in 1960, after a visit to the USA to collect the Freedom House Award, he had his passport confiscated because of his dangerously outspoken comments.†

South Africa

It is essential in reading *Cry, the Beloved Country* to have some detailed knowledge of the history and politics of South Africa. Although many of the themes of the novel are clearly universal and could occur in any serious literary work written in any language and set in any location (such themes, for example, as the difficulties of relationships between different members of the same family), there is a specifically South African political context upon which the novel is constantly drawing. Thus, whilst the work is certainly not provincial** in its concerns, it is undoubtedly a regional novel and can only be satisfactorily read with a knowledge of that region.

The principal fictional event in the novel, the murder of Arthur Jarvis, is described (Book Two, Chapter 5) as having taken place on

* For publication details of this and other works by Paton mentioned here, see Part 5.
† In addition to Paton's own autobiography, information about his life can be found in E. Callan, *Alan Paton*, Twayne, New York, 1968.
** See Callan, *Alan Paton*, p.97.

8 October 1946, but the novel draws upon a political context which includes not only real incidents in the period immediately preceding 1946 (as the author makes clear in his prefatory note), but also a whole history of conflict between black and white, between Dutch-speaking and English-speaking South Africans, and indeed between all the various ethnic groups which have lived in the country since the seventeenth century.

In Chapter 3 of the second book of *Cry, the Beloved Country* James Jarvis visits the house of his murdered son and finds, on the wall of his study, four pictures, including one of 'the white gabled house of Vergelegen'. In this single reference Alan Paton takes his readers back to the earliest point of contact between black Africans and white Europeans in this part of the continent, and to the beginnings of the conflict. Although the Portuguese, through Bartholomew Diaz, had been the first to reach the Cape of Good Hope in 1488, they had established no settlement there, and it was left to the Dutch East India Company to create a refreshment station on the Cape in 1652, in order to provide water, meat, vegetables and stores for ships of the company voyaging to and from the East. Soon after the establishment of this station Dutch families started to settle and farm the area, using slave labour to work the land. The picture of the white gabled house of Vergelegen symbolises the two faces of this early settlement, for Vergelegen was the farm of the Dutch commander of the station and it provided him with a luxurious way of life, but only at the expense of the oppressed slave population.

From the outset of European colonisation the settlers steadfastly refused to believe that the black Africans had any rights to the land, to their cattle, or to their own freedom; and one of the principal races of the Cape, the Bushmen, were removed almost entirely from the area, either shot or driven off in fear. Another major tribe, however, the Hottentots, remained on the Cape, and became assimilated into the European-dominated way of life, developing a modified version of the Dutch language called Afrikaans, and becoming labourers on the farms of the Europeans. Over the centuries the descendants of the Hottentots, and those descended from a mixture of Hottentot and European ancestry, have come to form the populous coloured community of the Cape district of South Africa. In this first phase of colonisation the Europeans adopted a mode of life very similar in principle to contemporary *apartheid*, which allowed Europeans and Africans to live alongside one another but in quite separate communities, having only the relationship of master and servant as their social intercourse. In this the Europeans were encouraged by their own particular brand of Christianity, Calvinism, which regarded certain people as predestined from birth to be allowed eternal salvation. Thus the Europeans were able to argue that they were the elect and the Africans the non-elect: their oppression was therefore given a religious sanction.

The Europeans were not, however, content to confine themselves to the area immediately surrounding the Cape. If the children of the settlers were to have large farms then new land needed to be annexed, and so the Dutch set off east to the fertile lands around the Great Fish River. Here they encountered a quite different African tribe, the Bantu or Zulu people, who were neither prepared to co-operate with the Europeans and work for them, as the Hottentots had done, nor to give up the land entirely, as the Bushmen had. Thus the Dutch farmers (or Boers as they were now known) came into conflict with the highly organised Zulu tribes and found that they were not allowed to continue their spread of colonisation indefinitely. The area which is now Natal was the location for these border wars and came to form the boundary of eastward colonisation.

At about the time when the wars between the Zulus and the Boers were starting, a further change was taking place in South Africa, for, at the end of the Napoleonic Wars, the British took over permanent control of the Cape, and their view of the proper relationship between themselves and the black population was very different from that of the Boers. Indeed many of the Boers felt so threatened by the British policy of equal opportunity for all races that they left the area of the Cape altogether to try to establish a republic of their own inland. Thus, by the middle of the nineteenth century, there were four European communities in South Africa: two British colonies at the Cape and in Natal; and two Boer republics on the Highlands around the Orange River (the Orange Free State Republic) and on the Transvaal grasslands (the South African Republic).

The Boer republics were both landlocked and were poorer than the British colonies. However, they were at least free to pursue their own independent system of government and of racial separation. The next event which was to bring the Boers and the English-speaking settlers into conflict was the discovery of mineral resources in the country: first diamonds and then gold. There was increasing competition about the ownership and exploitation of these two valuable commodities, leading eventually to war between the Boers and the British at the end of the nineteenth century. The British victory in this war enabled the establishment of a single united South Africa within the overall control of the British monarchy, and thus the Union of South Africa came into being in 1910. In the last seventy years the two most important political issues for South Africa have been the establishing of its political independence, free from any obligations to any European power, and the relationship within the country of black and white peoples. Both of these issues are crucial to *Cry, the Beloved Country*.

Whites and non-whites

Cry, the Beloved Country is told largely from the point of view of Stephen Kumalo, who is a member of a race referred to variously in the novel as African, Bantu, native, Zulu, black, and Kaffir. In contrast, the other principal racial group in the novel is referred to simply as European, and subdivided into two groups, Afrikaners and English-speaking. The use of these particular labels indicates something of the attitudes taken by the various characters to the different South African races. The term 'European' is particularly misleading since most white South Africans have never seen Europe and would not wish to live there. Arthur Jarvis, for example, was born on the farm which his grandfather had worked. In contrast to white settlers elsewhere on the African continent (and indeed elsewhere throughout the world), the colonists in South Africa came with the intention of becoming permanent residents, never returning to their homelands. The friction between the two groups of white South Africans is described below, but the label 'European' is particularly ironic in the light of the refusal of the Boer leader, Kruger, to allow recent immigrants from Europe to have any status in the Transvaal: thus the definition of who was European became one of the causes of the Boer War.*

There are paradoxes, too, inherent in the use of the term 'native' because, in a different context, it might be assumed that those described in this way had rights which emanated from their longer history of occupation; yet it is the claim of many white South Africans that the Bantu people have no such history. They claim that the Bantu came more recently to the south than the Dutch settlers, and they use this version of history to reinforce their claim that white domination of the country is legitimate. This is just one example of the kind of paradox which is fundamental to *Cry, the Beloved Country* and to much of the recent literature coming from South Africa. In all of this work a reader is aware very clearly of the ways in which history can be read very differently by different races, each interpreting events in a manner which suits their particular ideology. Some of the terms used in the novel to describe black South Africans are abusive and insulting, especially such a term as 'kaffir' which originally meant non-believer or infidel.† Alan Paton is fully attuned to the implications of the uses of these names and employs them quite deliberately to indicate the extent of the indifference of many white South Africans to their black countrymen. This indifference is particularly evident in the use of such impersonal and de-personalised expressions as 'labour costs' in Chapter 9 of the second book of the novel.

---

* See R. Segal, *The Race War*, Penguin Books, Harmondsworth, 1967, p.62.
† See Segal, *The Race War*, p.53, and Paton, *Towards the Mountain*, p.154.

South Africa changed during the nineteenth century from a land which was primarily agricultural (hence the use of the word 'Boer'* to describe the first European settlers) to an industrialised nation, and both agriculture and industry are vital to the economy of contemporary South Africa. Both systems are reflected in *Cry, the Beloved Country* and this is scarcely surprising, since Paton's own life has encompassed both urban and rural dwelling. As he moved from his post as a teacher in the rural Ixopo towards his position in the Diepkloof Reformatory in urban Johannesburg, Paton's literary preoccupations altered and his style broadened:

> It was one thing to delight in the peaceful beauty of the highlands of Natal, and to contrive fictional settings there; but it was quite a different thing to encounter the ugly realities confronting those, particularly Africans, who sought to adapt themselves to the new industrial world taking root in Africa (Callan, *Alan Paton*, p.41).

Many novels, written by black and white authors from all corners of the African continent, involve this contrast of a stable rural community which is on the wane and a bright, alluring urban centre to which many people, especially the young, are vulnerable.† In this respect the African novel of the mid-twentieth century bears a marked resemblance to the English novel of the late nineteenth century. This comparison, however, cannot be taken too far, for there are aspects of industrialisation particular to South Africa. For over a hundred and fifty years black Africans have been unable to move easily from one part of the country to another because of the imposition of 'pass laws'.** Originally these laws were designed to ensure that all black Africans in towns were in employment, and their entry into urban areas was regulated by the demands of white employers. However, with the expansion of the mining areas, further controls were progressively introduced until the only solution of the problem seemed to be the building of entirely separate compounds for the black workers in the mines. By the middle of the twentieth century it had become virtually impossible for a black South African to settle permanently in an urban community, because successive amendments to the pass laws had all but excluded African women entirely from the towns, and had thus denied the possibility of home life for the black urban workforce.

These laws have become a symbol of oppression and racism to black Africans. If the control of population intended by the pass laws is to be

* See L.E. Neame, *The History of Apartheid*, Pall Mall Press, London, 1962, p.11.
† For example, Chinua Achebe, *No Longer at Ease*, Heinemann, London, 1960.
** The fullest available account of the pass laws is contained in *The Oxford History of South Africa*, ed. M. Wilson and L. Thompson, Oxford University Press, London, 1971, pp.196–200.

achieved then constant checks have to be made by the police force, and this can do nothing to ease the tension between black workers and white police. At various times during the past forty years official committees have pointed with horror to the alarming numbers of black Africans being convicted for infringing pass laws: the number of pass law offences in the Transvaal alone between 1939 and 1941 was 273,790. Yet the laws stay in force and resentment continues to grow. As one white South African has recently written:

> Blacks had to carry pass books, special documents of identity of a remarkable complexity, and could be jailed for not being able to produce a pass correctly endorsed under all circumstances.*

One effect of the pass laws has been to increase the number of black 'criminals' and thus to fuel the white racist argument that blacks need to be kept under firm control. *Cry, the Beloved Country* includes among its many voices the expression of this kind of sentiment.

The attempt to control the black population extended into legislation about the kind of jobs a black African might be allowed to do. The successful exploitation of the mines of South Africa has relied almost entirely upon the exploitation of black labourers, recruited on short-term contracts, forced to live away from their families, and allowed to undertake only the most menial of labour in return for pitifully low wages. One of the first acts of the Union Parliament in 1911 was to pass the Mine and Works Act, which prevented black workers from obtaining skilled employment in the mines. It is against this background that the strikes by black miners must be placed. Ronald Segal describes official policy on the mines in the following terms:

> government found it more profitable to sell labour to the mines than invest sufficient resources to keep labour at home: the denial of skills and, above all, a natural family life to generations: these were the dividends paid to the Africans (*The Race War*, p.74).

Whilst the black males in the mining towns led miserable lives in the compounds, their families stayed on the land, and the position of rural black Africans deteriorated. As Stephen Kumalo comes to realise in the course of *Cry, the Beloved Country*, it is not entirely the weather or poor farming technique that is to blame for the failure of agriculture in Ndotsheni: it is also the lure of the city which deprives the country areas of the ablest workers.

In the period during and after the Second World War increasing numbers of black South Africans went to work in the booming industrial cities, yet found that they had nowhere to live. The building of

* D. Woods, *Biko*, Paddington Press, London, 1978, p.43.

Shanty Town described in Chapter 9 of the first book of *Cry, the Beloved Country* is based very firmly upon the historical fact of post-war South Africa:

> Most of the non-European 'dormitories' throughout the Union suffered from overcrowding and rack-renting, because the Africans and the Coloured owners of stands (freehold plots) mortgaged them heavily, as a rule to European individuals or Building Societies, and then sought to meet their liabilities by packing in far too many tenants. Nor could the inhabitants readily find homes elsewhere, as the 15,000 folk who marched out of swarming Orlando and Alexandra under the leadership of Mpanza Sofazonka, discovered when they tried to found Moroka on the opposite hillside. The Labour Johannesburg City Council promptly sent policemen to pull down the shacks and only deigned to recognise the new shanty town after the crowd, led by its womenfolk, had stoned the hated invaders and killed two of them.*

The authorities were able to exercise a further mode of control over black Africans in urban areas through their manipulation of the transport system. The black Africans could be kept in poverty by the charging of high fares on the buses: it would be impossible to avoid paying the increased fares since many of the dormitory areas for black workers were far away from their places of work. The bus strike which Stephen Kumalo encounters in Johannesburg is based upon real events: there were two boycotts of the buses by black workers during the Second World War, spurred on by prohibitive increases in fares. Here is an account of a later strike in 1957 which echoes uncannily the description in Paton's novel almost a decade earlier:

> African workers decided to walk to and from their work rather than pay an increased bus fare that had been sanctioned by the Road Transportation Board.... Police harassed the walking Africans by demanding to see their passes and, when they were given lifts by sympathetic Europeans (a common occurrence), by stopping the cars on the pretence of searching for wanted men or for permits... something like 45,000 Africans walked distances of 18 to 20 miles a day, and kept it up for ten weeks until the Chamber of Commerce and the Johannesburg City Council intervened.†

* Eric A. Walker, *A History of Southern Africa*, Longman, London, 1962, p.757.
† L. Marquard, *The Peoples and Policies of South Africa*, Oxford University Press, London, 1960, pp.151–2.

Boers and British

Racial conflict in South Africa is by no means confined to the friction between black and white: there are also wide divisions within the community between those of Dutch descent and those whose ancestors were British. The divisions can be exemplified partly through the terms used by the two groups to describe phenomena they have in common: South Africans of Dutch descent have described themselves for over a hundred years as Afrikaners, whereas their English-speaking compatriots continue to refer to them by the contemptuous term 'Boer', which implies not only 'farmer' but also 'peasant', since the term was originally used to describe the servants of the East India Company.* Similarly, the war between the two groups at the end of the nineteenth century is called by British historians the Boer War, which might be taken to imply that it was the Boers who were responsible for the outbreak of war: Afrikaners call it The English War.

Even after the Act of Union in 1910 it would have been strange if two peoples who had so recently been at war should suddenly settle down to live amicably with one another. In fact a peculiar situation has developed in which Afrikaners and English-speaking South Africans are now divided not only geographically and in terms of their attitude to black Africans and to Europe, but also in linguistic and in economic terms. After Union there was a real danger that the Afrikaners might lose their own separate identity and become submerged and anglicised. This danger was partially manifest through attitudes to language:

> The English language, with an established international position, was, and to a certain . . . extent still is, the language of trade and commerce, of the professions, of amusement and recreation, and of urban society. The urge to learn English, and the temptation to regard it as the only cultured language were strong, and there was at one time a tendency among Afrikaners with pretensions to a more 'polite' way of living to look down on Afrikaans as . . . something of which to be slightly ashamed (Marquard, *The Peoples and Policies of South Africa*, p.68).

This preference for one language rather than the other has had significant consequences in terms of the foreign policy of the country and its expression of allegiance to Europe. It has also affected the reception of the ideas of South Aricans outside their country. Although it may be necessary to explain in a work such as this some of the political background, Paton's novel can nevertheless be read by a wide audience all over the world because it is written in English. A non-English-speaking South African writer faces a much more severe problem:

* See Neame, *The History of Apartheid*, p.11.

For writers whose medium is Afrikaans or any of the African ver-
naculars, the problem of provincialism is additionally acute, since
their potential audience may be fewer in numbers than the population of a medium-sized British or American city. To the world at
large, therefore, South African literature is represented by the work
of those poets and novelists of whatever racial background who
write in English (Callan, *Alan Paton*, p.97).

Deprived in this respect of the opportunity of placing their views
before an international audience, it is scarcely surprising that the more
extreme Afrikaners should have become isolationist and reactionary.
It is ironic too that these reactionary views have led Afrikaners on the
one hand to dominate South African politics since the Union and yet
on the other to lose economic control of the country to the numerically
smaller English-speaking South Africans:

> the majority of Afrikaans farmers are not progressive. A long tradi-
> tion of large farms easily acquired, the presence of a relatively abun-
> dant supply of 'cheap' labour, and a contempt for 'experts' have
> induced bad economic habits and retarded scientific farming
> (Marquard, *The Peoples and Policies of South Africa*, p.71).

This division of political and economic control between the
Afrikaners and the British has led some commentators on South
African affairs to conclude that the economic success of the English-
speaking South Africans has caused them to turn a blind eye to the
anti-democratic aims of Afrikaner nationalists, although remaining in
theory opposed to such aims.*

However, division of control has not prevented the continuation of
conflict between the two races. It came into the open again over the
question of whether South Africa should enter the Second World War,
a war regarded by Afrikaners as an English war and therefore no concern of theirs. South Africa did eventually enter the war on the British
side, and Alan Paton has written eloquently about the effects of this
decision in his second novel, *Too Late the Phalarope*. In some respects
this novel deals with the problems of South Africa on a more sophisti-
cated level than *Cry, the Beloved Country*, which has resulted in its
being given less attention than the earlier novel. Its central character is
an Afrikaner policeman who nevertheless decides to fight in the Second
World War:

> He took the red oath, which meant that he would go anywhere in
> Africa, and they gave him red flashes to put on his shoulders. But
> the red oath, to those who would not take it, meant only one thing,

---

* See M. Banton, *Race Relations*, Tavistock, London, 1967, p.172.

that the wearer of it was a Smuts man, a traitor to the language and struggle of the Afrikaner people, and a lickspittle of the British Empire and the English King, fighting in an English war that no true Afrikaner would take part in (*Too Late the Phalarope*, p.35).

The policeman's father, an Afrikaner patriarchal figure, disowns his son twice in the novel, once for consorting with a black African girl and, on an earlier occasion, for fighting in the war:

> he had acquired a tolerance for dancing, and for Englishmen so long as they did not talk of England as home; .... And when his son Pieter took the red oath and had gone to the war, he would bear no mention of his name, but had restored him to favour when Holland fell, not because he had any special love for Holland, but because it was a small nation, as the Transvaal had been in 1899 (*Too Late the Phalarope*, p.90).

The intolerance which Jakob van Vlaanderen shows towards his son is a classic instance of that conflict which one commentator has identified as the most bitter of all the tensions in South Africa:

> The bitterest enmity exists, not between Afrikaner and English, but between Afrikaner and Afrikaner . . . the cause of this bitterness lies in the difference of attitude towards England and English-speaking South Africans (Marquard, *op. cit.*, p.71).

Isolation and ignorance

There has been continuous international opposition to South Africa's *apartheid* policy since its inception in 1948. This opposition has taken the form of repeated criticism at the United Nations Organisation, especially from representatives of black African states. In 1960 a slim majority of white South Africans decided that it would be to their advantage to become a republic and thus to escape being ousted from power by black nationalists, as had happened elsewhere in Africa. However, South Africa was not to be allowed to become a republic and yet to stay within the Commonwealth as India had; such was the force of Commonwealth opposition to *apartheid* that the new republic ceased to be a member.

Since becoming a republic South Africa has found friends hard to come by. Opposition to its policies has taken the form of the banning of sporting contests between representative sides from South Arica and those from other countries, particularly Commonwealth teams. However, even such moves as these have not always had their intended effect and have revealed aspects of the ignorance which the outside world still has about conditions in South Africa. For example, it is not generally appreciated that white South Africans are as divided in their sport as in most other aspects of their lives. Afrikaners are passionately interested in rugby (a fact which Alan Paton makes great use of in *Too Late the Phalarope*), but have no interest in cricket, the favourite game of the English-speaking South Africans. Thus, to be truly effective, a sporting boycott would need to be mounted very selectively.

More alarming, however, than the ignorance of the outside world of the political situation within South Africa is the ignorance of South Africans themselves of the ideologies and life-styles of their compatriots. Writing of the reception of *Cry, the Beloved Country* Alan Paton notes:

> Some people thought it was propagandist, political, polemical. The vast majority of these people were white South Africans. The reason they disliked the novel was that it revealed a picture of South Africa that they did not wish to look at. They disliked the film based on the book also. I sat next to Mrs D.F. Malan, wife of our Prime Minister from 1948 to 1954, at the premiere of the film; she was clearly disturbed and said to me, 'Surely, Mr Paton, you don't really think things are like that.' I said to her, 'Madam, I lived in that world for thirteen years', but I did not add, 'and you, Madam, have never seen anything of it at all'(*Towards the Mountain*, p.272).

Paton, more perhaps than any other South African, has tried to see as much as he possibly could of the various lives of the different tribes of South Africa. He learned Afrikaans and his attempt to understand the Afrikaner position led him to join in the centenary celebration of the Great Trek in December 1938. Even though this experience ultimately brought about his disenchantment with the extreme form of Malan's Afrikaner nationalism, he was at least able to reject this viewpoint from the stance of one who had thoroughly attempted to understand it. The voices in his fiction are those of black Africans, of Afrikaners, of Jews, Indians, and of Coloureds. As yet, however, the voice of his own people, of the concerned white liberal, has not been given full tongue in his writing. Perhaps the final two parts of the trilogy started by *Ah, But Your Land is Beautiful* will fill this gap.

A note on the text

Cry, the Beloved Country was first published in 1948 by Scribners, New York, and in the same year by Jonathan Cape, London. The references in these notes are to the edition of the novel published by Penguin Books, Harmondsworth, in 1958. These references are always to chapters rather than to pages, so the reader should have no difficulty in using these Notes whatever edition is used.

Part 2

Summaries
of CRY, THE BELOVED COUNTRY

General summary

The Reverend Stephen Kumalo, a black South African, is parson in the village of Ndotsheni. His brother John, sister Gertrude, and son Absalom, have all left the village many years before to live in Johannesburg, and neither Stephen nor his wife has heard from them. One day Stephen receives a letter from a fellow-clergyman in Johannesburg who has met Gertrude and asks Stephen to come to her as soon as possible. Stephen goes to the city full of hope that he will be able to find all of his family again and reunite them in Ndotsheni.

Although he is duped on the way to the Mission House he receives a warm welcome from the Reverend Msimangu and the two men set out to locate Stephen's relatives. Msimangu has warned Stephen in advance that his sister Gertrude is living an immoral life, and the girl seems to be genuinely pleased at the prospect of leaving Johannesburg and returning to Ndotsheni with her small son. Stephen persuades her to leave her room at once and stay in lodgings with him until they go home.

Stephen finds that his brother John, as well as running a successful shop, has become a prominent political figure. However, when Stephen and Msimangu visit the shop, they find that John's moral standards have declined and that his wife has left him. They nevertheless discover their first clue in the search for Absalom, for he has been friendly with John's son, and John gives them an address where he believes the two boys to be working. However, after several days of searching throughout the city the two men find that Absalom has been leading a life of crime and that the trail eventually leads them to the reformatory. Here they discover that Absalom has recently been released so that he can marry the girl who is having his child. Stephen's joy is quickly turned to despair when he traces the girl only to find that Absalom has deserted her.

Stephen decides that it is his duty to care for the girl, but he suspends his quest for a few days and visits an institution for the blind with Msimangu. On their return they discover that the police are looking for Absalom, and Stephen suspects that it is in connection with the shooting of a white South African called Jarvis, whose father lives at Notsheni. The young man from the reformatory arrives to confirm

Stephen's fears and to take him to see his son in prison. On the way Stephen calls to see his brother to explain that his son has also been arrested, together with another boy. However, after the two men have spoken to their sons, John Kumalo is convinced that he needs only to hire a good lawyer and his son will go free. In his despair Stephen is comforted by a white priest, Father Vincent, and also by the innocence and charm of the young girl who is carrying his grandchild, and who passionately wishes to accompany him back to Ndotsheni. However, Mrs Lithebe, in whose house Stephen and his family are staying, has some misgivings about the influence which Gertrude might be having on the young girl.

The second book opens, like the first, in Ndotsheni, but with the focus upon James Jarvis, the father of the man murdered by Absalom Kumalo. Jarvis and his wife fly to Johannesburg immediately upon receiving the news of the murder of their son and they stay with the Harrisons, the family of their son's wife. From reading typescripts written by his son, and by talking to his friend John Harrison, James Jarvis learns a great deal about his son's liberal opinions and the beliefs behind them. Jarvis and Stephen Kumalo meet by accident in Johannesburg and, after a difficult conversation, Stephen reveals that it was his son who murdered Arthur Jarvis. He is relieved when James replies that he feels no anger towards him.

Absalom Kumalo is found guilty of murder, and the judge can find no reason for clemency: he sentences him to death. The two other boys, however, are acquitted because of insufficient evidence. Before leaving for Ndotsheni, Stephen sees his son married in prison by Father Vincent and hears from Msimangu that he intends to enter a closed community. Msimangu gives all his worldly possessions to Stephen. On the morning when they are all due to leave for Ndotsheni Stephen finds that Gertrude has disappeared.

In the third book Stephen returns to Ndotsheni unsure whether he can continue there. However, the people are delighted to see him, and his sister's son and his daughter-in-law make themselves at home in his house. Stephen becomes friendly with the young grandson of James Jarvis, and finds to his astonishment that Jarvis has decided to do all in his power to improve the village. He plans to build a dam, provides milk for the children in time of drought, and hires an agricultural demonstrator to teach the villagers how to get more out of the land. Meanwhile the two men sustain one another through times of personal crisis: the death of Mrs Jarvis, and the dreadful night when Stephen Kumalo, his son having been denied any mercy, waits for the moment of Absalom's execution.

Detailed summaries
BOOK ONE

Chapter 1

This chapter presents two contrasting descriptions of the South African scenery: the rich and fertile land of the white farmer, and the over-worked land of the black Africans.

NOTES AND GLOSSARY:
from Ixopo into the hills: Paton describes his reaction to the beauty of Ixopo in *Towards the Mountain*, pp.84–5
beyond any singing of it: beyond any description
matted: closely interwoven
The soil cannot keep them any more: this phrase recurs throughout the novel and emphasises the link between the people and the land itself

Chapter 2

The Reverend Stephen Kumalo receives a letter from a parson in Johannesburg which informs him that his sister Gertrude is ill and asks him to come at once. The chapter introduces the Kumalo family and describes economically the sense of loss felt by the parson and his wife at the way in which Gertrude, Stephen's brother John, and their only son Absalom have all left them for Johannesburg. Stephen and his wife are forced to use all their savings in order to finance Stephen's trip.

NOTES AND GLOSSARY:
Go well: the formal farewell which recurs throughout the novel
as a Zulu who reads English: the letter would be written in English as the standard language of formal communication
This money was to send Absalom to St Chad's: we have already been told that Absalom has disappeared to Johannesburg yet his father has persisted in pretending that he will return and that money will be needed to send him to college
they are lost: in both a physical and moral sense

Chapter 3

Stephen begins his journey and is given a message at the station from a man who seeks news of a girl in Johannesburg.

NOTES AND GLOSSARY:
agapanthus ... poker: varieties of flowers
wattles: trees or shrubs of the acacia family
uSmith: Paton attempts in the novel to convey the Zulu pronunciation of English names
it is always so: Stephen says this in order to impress the other passengers and to make them believe that he is accustomed to travelling to Johannesburg

Chapter 4

After a lengthy journey Stephen arrives in Johannesburg. He is cheated by a young man at the bus station, but eventually arrives at the house of the Reverend Msimangu in Sophiatown.

NOTES AND GLOSSARY:
a train that has no engine: an electric train
water comes out of a bottle ... over again: this a description of an advertisement

Chapter 5

Kumalo has dinner with Msimangu and a group of priests. They talk of the problems of life, both in the country and in the city. After the meal Kumalo and Msimangu talk privately and Stephen asks for news of his family. Msimangu takes him to the house of Mrs Lithebe where he is to stay.

NOTES AND GLOSSARY:
In Johannesburg? Everywhere it is so: one function of this chapter is to establish that the problems of the city are linked with and caused by those in the rural communities
I have another great sorrow: Stephen is careful to present his problems formally and gradually. It would not be appropriate or polite for him to explain all his problems in a single burst

Chapter 6

Stephen and Msimangu go to Claremont to look for Gertrude. Stephen finds her and brings her and her child to Mrs Lithebe's house.

NOTES AND GLOSSARY:
the names there are very beautiful: it is ironic that so squalid a place should have beautiful street names

I had no money to write: even at this stage Gertrude's replies are evasive and unconvincing

Where shall I sleep?: Stephen manages to shame Gertrude by making her realise that she cannot expect her brother to stay with her in such a place

the tribe was being rebuilt: this is Stephen's aim, but he must learn that the tribe cannot be rebuilt as it was

---

Chapter 7

Having bought new clothes for Gertrude and her child, Stephen sets out with Msimangu to visit his brother John. He finds that John is not living with his wife and that he feels more comfortable in the city where he is free from the customs and restraints of the village. John gives Stephen the address of a factory where he believes Absalom to be working, but the boy is not to be found there, nor is he at the address given by one of the workers.

NOTES AND GLOSSARY:

a stipend of eight pounds a month: this may be compared with the money earned by John Kumalo's business

Good morning, my brother: John interprets this merely as the greeting of one friend to another

He is a trick . . . to hold together: John Kumalo does not speak in lies. He is right to identify social injustices, but wrong to feel that these excuse immorality

Our customs are different here: Msimangu is shrewd in observing that John Kumalo's way of life is not built upon any system of tradition or custom

we did not meet any more: in the city the bonds of family are not strong enough to allow members of the same family to protect one another as they would in the country

There is something like discomfort in John's eyes: John is the first character we have met in the book who has known Absalom since the boy has been in Johannesburg. His discomfort is a forewarning that Absalom is in trouble

this is not the way to get to Doornfontein: throughout the book characters are torn, as Msimangu is here, between the wish for a long-term solution for the problems of the country and the need for some immediate action in their own lives

Chapter 8

Kumalo and Msimangu set off the following morning to try to trace Absalom. They are persuaded not to take a bus because there is a boycott over fare increases. A white man gives them a lift part of the way in his car. There is, however, no sign of Absalom in Alexandra, and the people he knew show fear at the mention of his name. Eventually a taxi-driver suggests that they look in the shanties of Orlando, and they take a taxi home again.

NOTES AND GLOSSARY:

All these buses go to Johannesburg: like the transport systems of many cities, the bus routes serve primarily to carry passengers to and from work

Our business is very urgent: again there is a conflict between personal and public needs

One of our young boys snatched a bag: the increasing references to crime in this section of the novel prepare us for the fate of Absalom Kumalo

Something touched him: throughout this chapter there are references to an embarrassed co-operation between whites and blacks

food in bottles: bottled food would generally be the food of white South Africans and hence in these circumstances might be assumed to have been stolen

You see the bicycles: the whole chapter is carefully constructed to balance Stephen's personal quest against larger political issues. Thus it begins and ends with the boycott of the buses

That is what beats me: Msimangu is astonished that the white man can risk being taken to court: a black African would be arrested immediately. The situation in actual bus boycotts in Johannesburg is described in Part 1 of these Notes

Chapter 9

This descriptive chapter does not concern itself directly with the main narrative of Stephen Kumalo's quest, although it is clearly relevant to it, and refers to Dubula, a character introduced in the previous chapter. It is concerned with the difficulties encountered by those trying to find housing in Johannesburg, especially those arriving from the outlying areas.

NOTES AND GLOSSARY:

there is work in Johannesburg: this opening paragraph presents an idealised portrait of the city, a view held by those who have never been there and who feel it a place where all wrongs can be put right

Yes, I have a room that I could let: the speaker of this passage is presented as a person of upright morals and traditional values, struggling against financial hardship

I do not like this woman: the effect of overcrowding forces people to be suspicious of each other. There is not the trust of the rural community

You are only a child on the list: your name has not been on the list for any length of time

Quietly my child ... your mother is by you: here and elsewhere in the novel the mother figure is a symbol of the country as a whole, a loving Africa watching helplessly as her children die

They take photographs: the effect of publicity (contrived by Dubula) is to bring a temporary alleviation of the situation. The historical facts of the building of shanty towns are alluded to in Part 1 of these Notes

Chapter 10

Kumalo and Msimangu go to Shanty Town and discover that Absalom has been sent to a reformatory. A young white man at the reformatory tells them that Absalom has been released for a month in order to marry the girl who is having his baby. However, when they reach the girl's house, they find that Absalom has been missing for several days, and the girl seems reconciled to the fact that he will not return. After a bitter outburst from Msimangu on the futility of the quest, Stephen and he agree that it must continue, and that they must care for the girl.

NOTES AND GLOSSARY:

he would tell him of the great valley: throughout his stay in the city Stephen is able to move others by his descriptions of his homeland. The countryside has a beauty which the city lacks

Yea, though I walk through the valley ... with me: this reference to the Bible, to the 23rd Psalm, introduces a new comparison. In the previous chapter Stephen's search was contrasted with the wider political struggle. Here the context is not political but religious

The reformatory: Paton's description of this institution is drawn from his own experience as Principal of the Diepkloof Reformatory just outside Johannesburg. Reformatories were not introduced in South Africa until 1934 (see Alan Paton, *Towards the Mountain*, p.132)

would have stumbled: Kumalo is overcome with grief

there are thousands such in Johannesburg: this speech shows the difference between Msimangu and Kumalo. For Kumalo the quest is a personal venture; Msimangu cannot see it as a unique or special event

it is my work, but it is his son: the young man can appreciate that the quest has a deeper significance for Kumalo than it can ever have for him

Chapter 11

Msimangu persuades Kumalo that he should suspend the search for a while in order to get some rest. At dinner a white priest brings in a newspaper which carries the report of a murder. The murdered man, Arthur Jarvis, was born in Ndotsheni and Kumalo is very affected by the report.

NOTES AND GLOSSARY:

a small bright boy: the death of Jarvis is made the more poignant by the fact that he is remembered not only as a man who had done great service but also as one who had been a child of South Africa

At 1.30 p.m. today: the style of this paragraph is that of a newspaper report

Here in my heart . . . nothing but fear: Stephen is deeply afraid that his son may be implicated in the murder of Arthur Jarvis

Chapter 12

This chapter combines general description with a further development in the narrative. The first half is a kaleidoscope of attitudes to crime, education, and segregation, expressed by the voices of reactionaries and liberals. In the second half of the chapter Msimangu is visited by Mrs Ndlela who tells him that the police have been to her, asking questions about Absalom. Kumalo and Msimangu retrace their steps on their quest and find that the police have visited all the other people who knew Absalom, including the girl who was to have been his wife.

NOTES AND GLOSSARY:

who can enjoy the seventy years: seventy years (three score years and ten) is the traditional lifespan as mentioned in the Bible

There are voices crying what must be done: the rest of the first section of this chapter consists of various voices crying out. However, these voices are not in agreement

It's a crying scandal, ladies and gentlemen: this speech is in the style of an orator addressing a public meeting

I say we shall always have native crime: this speaker is of a more liberal viewpoint than the previous voice

pass-laws: laws controlling the movement of black Africans from one area to another. The details of these laws are outlined in Part 1 of these Notes

We went to the Zoo Lake, my dear: this speaker is not part of the public meeting which has been going on so far in this chapter. The voice is that of a woman talking to a friend at the Tennis Club

Get your racquet, my dear: the way in which this conversation is terminated is a travesty of the pressing issues which prevent political debate elsewhere in the novel. Here tennis takes priority

We shall live from day to day: in this fine paragraph there is an implicit comment on the nature of freedom. The whites live in such fear that they have no real freedom at all, despite their wealth and power

They are holding a meeting in Parkwold: this paragraph effects the transition from general description back to the narrative of Stephen Kumalo by re-introducing the murder of Arthur Jarvis

heavy matters: serious, illegal affairs

but there is fear, not eagerness in his voice: Kumalo is about to embark on a re-enactment of his search for Absalom, but he sets off this time without hope

it was now, now, that he went: he left very recently

Chapter 13

This chapter is principally concerned with the thoughts of Stephen Kumalo on his visit to the institution for the blind at Ezenzeleni. Here he has time to think about the fate of his son, his sister, and his grandchild who has yet to be born. He is also inspired by the sermon which Msimangu preaches to the blind, which Stephen thinks to have been addressed to him alone.

NOTES AND GLOSSARY:
some rising of the spirit: there are two events in this chapter which affect Kumalo. He is moved here by the very sight of the land, and later in the chapter by the sermon from Msimangu

when he sits in a place of ashes and destruction: Kumalo is moved to contemplation because of the difficulty of his present circumstances

The tribe was broken: this is a turning point in Kumalo's career within the novel, for his entire aim so far has been to rebuild the tribe. He now no longer believes that this is possible

osiers: young shoots of willow

vestments: the ceremonial clothing of a priest

I the lord have called thee: this passage is a quotation from the Bible, Isaiah, 42. The later text is from Isaiah, 40

minister to: take care of the spiritual and physical welfare of

he is despised by some: this sentence introduces a paragraph which brings together the political, personal and religious elements in the narrative

I have tried every way to touch you: in his humility Msimangu denies that he has been responsible for moving Kumalo. He claims that it is the passage from Isaiah which has effected the recovery

Chapter 14

Stephen Kumalo has returned from Ezenzeleni and is watching his sister selling her possessions when Msimangu and the young man from the reformatory arrive. They tell him that Absalom has been found and that he has been arrested for the murder of Arthur Jarvis. Since Stephen's nephew was with Absalom and has also been arrested, he goes to break the news to his brother John, and they visit their sons in prison. Stephen is unable to obtain from his son any explanation either about this particular crime or about the life that he has led in Johannesburg. When he leaves Absalom, Stephen finds that his brother John is anxious to hire a lawyer to try to prove that his son was not present at the scene of the crime. The young man from the reformatory, who was brought them to the prison, drives off in disgust at John Kumalo's attitude, and Stephen is left in despair, determined to seek the help of Father Vincent.

NOTES AND GLOSSARY:
the black people do not buy such pots and pans: the implication here is

that the goods have been stolen from the house of a
white person

As though they did not know: unconsciously, by instinct

what he said: what his nodding meant

the prodigal: the prodigal son; a reference to the parable of the prodigal son who eventually returns home to be welcomed and forgiven by his father. It is told in the Bible, Luke, 15

now I shall see him go out: the young man predicts that Absalom will be sentenced to death for his crime

Chapter 15

Kumalo returns to his lodgings and is visited by the man from the reformatory who has come to apologise for his harsh words at the prison. The young man warns him not to trust his brother John, and advises Stephen to hire a lawyer for his own son. He feels that the fact that Absalom did not intend to harm Jarvis might work in his favour. The two men go to seek Father Vincent's advice on the matter and, when the young man has gone, Kumalo reveals the depth of his despair to the priest. Although Father Vincent finds the interview a difficult one, he is able to provide some comfort for Kumalo and offers to take responsibility himself for Absalom's reform.

NOTES AND GLOSSARY:

something that is himself: true to his own feelings of anger

I felt . . . : Kumalo was going to describe the despair he had felt

the truth and nothing but the truth: this phrase is taken from the oath which is sworn by all giving evidence in the courts of Britain and of many other countries. Its significance here is the implication that John Kumalo's concern will not be with the truth, but with freeing his son at all costs

hoping that this would soon be finished: one of the strengths of this chapter is that it presents a portrait of Father Vincent as a fallible and human priest, disturbed and unhappy about the task he has to perform

It was revealed to others to whom it did not matter: this telling line expresses one of the most important messages in the novel. Families are breaking up and only families can give the care necessary to keep control of wayward adolescents

that symbolic language: the parables of the Christian religion
There was a thief upon the cross: an allusion to the thief who was
crucified at the same time as Christ (see the Bible,
Luke, 23)
He will repent: Stephen is suspicious that Absalom will make only
a token repentance, that he will repent with his
mouth but not with his heart
Pray for Gertrude: the words of Father Vincent provide the dynamic
for the rest of the novel, which is to be concerned
with the ways in which Kumalo can restore life
back in Ndotsheni

Chapter 16

Stephen goes to Pimville, to the girl who is having his son's baby. He
asks her whether she wants to marry Absalom and to go with him,
Stephen, to Ndotsheni. She agrees very willingly and Kumalo leaves
her, finding to his surprise that she has made him laugh.

NOTES AND GLOSSARY:
I do not wish to take ... unwillingly: it is at this point that the girl
begins to feel a real desire to marry Absalom. She
wishes to be adopted into the family of Stephen
Kumalo
in the school: at the reformatory
Have you had a murderer before?: this unusually harsh sentence is
both an expression of Stephen's strength of feeling
and a preparation for the wild thought which is to
follow

Chapter 17

Kumalo asks Mrs Lithebe whether he can bring back the girl to her
house and she agrees. Mrs Lithebe takes care to instruct the girl on how
to behave and to warn her against indecorous laughter with Gertrude.
Stephen has another interview with his son in prison and talks to him
about the forthcoming marriage. He returns to the Mission House
where Father Vincent introduces him to the lawyer Mr Carmichael,
who accepts Absalom's case without asking for a fee.

NOTES AND GLOSSARY:
on the floor of a decent house, than to ...: Stephen would have
continued 'than to sleep in a bed in a dissolute
house', but Mrs Lithebe makes it clear that she
understands

it is the careless laughter that she does not like: Gertrude's tendency to sinful laughter was referred to in Chapter 6. This episode prepares us for the fact that Gertrude will not go back to Ndotsheni

it is your time to be careful: the girl needs to be careful because she is pregnant

You mean . . . the law?: this is a heavily ironic sentence because Stephen knows that his son's friends were none of the things he describes

pro deo: (*Latin*) for God

BOOK TWO

Chapter 1

Book Two opens in a manner identical to the opening of Book One, with a description of the Umzimkulu valley. This time, however, the climax of the description is not Ndotsheni but the farm of James Jarvis. The chapter takes us back to the afternoon of Arthur Jarvis's murder and describes the way in which the news is broken to his father and mother.

NOTES AND GLOSSARY:

what there is to see: Jarvis is looking out for a sign of a rain cloud; ironically, what he is to see is the car bringing news of his son's death

kaffir path: rough footpath

if these people had only learned: the reactionary whites in the novel always refer to the black Africans as 'these people'

but his life was his own: this is an ironic observation since we know that Arthur Jarvis's life is already over

a decent fellow for an Afrikaner: this paragraph neatly conveys the antipathy between English-speaking South Africans and Afrikaners. For further discussion of this issue see Part 1 of these Notes

There's still that to do: he has yet to break the news to Arthur's mother

Chapter 2

The Jarvises arrive in Johannesburg and are looked after by the Harrisons, the family of Arthur Jarvis's wife. After seeing the body in the mortuary Mr Jarvis has a conversation with Mr Harrison in which he learns of the political and social convictions of his son.

NOTES AND GLOSSARY:

lingo: language
pipe down: keep quiet
not my food and drink: not someone I want to be familiar with
missionaries: the word is normally applied to those whose mission is to spread the Christian faith among people who have not encountered it before. However, Jarvis is using the word here in a more literal sense, applying it to the political mission which his son had
ineluctable: inescapable

Chapter 3

James Jarvis visits his son's house and, among the papers he sees on his desk, he finds the manuscript of the essay which his son was writing at the time of his death.

NOTES AND GLOSSARY:

Toc H: an organisation formed during the First World War comprised of young men pledged to help one another and to study social conditions. The movement spread to South Africa in 1926 and Alan Paton describes his own involvement in it in *Towards the Mountain*, pp.103−6. He was Honorary Commissioner for Toc H in Southern Africa from 1949 to 1954
Abraham Lincoln: 1809−65, a President of the United States and a campaigner against slavery
Vergelegen: a rich farm east of Capetown which was the residence of the early Dutch commanders of the Cape station in the late seventeenth century
Life of Rhodes: Cecil Rhodes (1853−1902) became Prime Minister of the Cape Colony in 1890. He was devoted to the northward expansion of the colony and eventually founded Rhodesia in 1890. In the later years of his life he was passionately involved in developing railways in the southern half of Africa
Smuts: Field-Marshal Jan Christiaan Smuts (1870−1950) was an outstanding Afrikaner commander during the Boer War (1899−1902) who afterwards worked for friendship with the British. He was Prime Minister of the Union from 1939 to 1948
Life of Louis Botha: Louis Botha (1862−1919) was the first Prime Minister of the South African Union

'The Famous Speech at Gettysburg': Abraham Lincoln delivered an address on 19 November 1863 to dedicate a national cemetery on the site of a Civil War battlefield at Gettysburg, Pennsylvania, USA. The speech combines the two themes of personal sorrow at the loss of life and the hope for national democracy

the fatal passage: the corridor where Arthur Jarvis was killed

---

Chapter 4

After Arthur Jarvis's funeral his father talks to Mr Harrison about the political situation in the country. The following morning Harrison brings him the final pages of his son's manuscript, including the very page he wrote before he was killed. Jarvis is moved by his reading of these final words and finds that his wife is equally touched when she reads them.

NOTES AND GLOSSARY:

the furnace . . . ashes: Arthur Jarvis's body is cremated

wind up Arthur's affairs: settle the outstanding matters of business and administration

string 'em all up: hang them all

Our girl's husband comes in: Harrison is aware of the irony of this speech. He is depicting himself as a tolerant and liberal employer, and yet the system within which he operates makes it normal for husbands and wives to be separated

sanitary lanes: gulleys into which human waste would be thrown in the days before an efficient sewage system had been established

loafers: vagabonds, vagrants

square deal: fair treatment

subsidies: grants from the government

soaks the mines: taxes the mines

the goose stops laying the eggs: an allusion to the popular European folk-tale of the goose which laid golden eggs

if we ever get a republic: in fact South Africa became a republic after a referendum of its white citizens in 1960

Nationalists: those Afrikaners in favour of South Africa breaking ties with Great Britain and becoming an independent republic

old garden-boy: former gardener

hew wood and draw water: perform only menial tasks. The enemies of the Israelites were subjugated in this way (see the Bible, Joshua, 9)

Second Inaugural Address: the speech made by the President of the United States at the beginning of his second term of office on 4 March 1865. Its most memorable passage speaks of: 'malice toward none: with charity for all; with firmness in the right, as God gives us to see the right'. Lincoln, like Arthur Jarvis, was killed by a gunman

Chapter 5

The trial of Absalom Kumalo and his two friends begins. Absalom is cross-examined and admits that what he did was wrong.

NOTES AND GLOSSARY:
is a high seat: throughout the chapters which describe the trial, the present tense is used. The reasons for this are discussed in Part 3 of these Notes
the King: the King of England
like a lamp ... in the house: this is a good example of the way in which Paton's style mirrors the language of the Bible
It had been blessed: the implication behind the blessing of this bar, as with the voice which had instructed Johannes Parfuri, is that the three boys have been involved in a pagan ceremony

Chapter 6

This descriptive chapter gives an account of the reactions to the discovery of a new goldfield in the Orange Free State.

NOTES AND GLOSSARY:
Odendaalsrust: gold was discovered here in 1946
nothing to wonder at: not very competent
Hofmeyr: there were two famous South Africans called Jan Hofmeyr. The first Jan Hofmeyr (1845–1909) was a friend of Rhodes; the second, his nephew (1894–1948), was a progressive politician whose biography was written by Alan Paton. It is this second Jan Hofmeyr who is alluded to here
there is a place ... already: Hofmeyr is a town to the north-east of Capetown which was named in honour of the elder Jan Hofmeyr in 1912
unpronounceable names: this whole chapter is written from the point of view of an English-speaking South African who despises his Afrikaner compatriots

into our beards: secretly, in private
United Party: a political party formed in 1934 as a coalition between English-speaking and Afrikaner whites
Rhodes or Stellenbosch: two of the universities of South Africa
burns bright in the forests of the night: a quotation from the poem 'Tyger' by William Blake (1757–1827)
determined solely by mining costs: the argument presented here is flawed because it fails to include wages as part of mining costs
has a lot of kick in it: is still likely to rise in price
saves art from dying out: this is a subtle piece of irony from Paton. The speaker here appears to believe that art can be kept alive solely through capital
they shoot game and feel at one with Nature: again an ironic sentence. These hunters commune with nature by destroying it
Tennessee Vally Authority: a project established by President Roosevelt in the USA as part of his 'New Deal' politics in the 1930s. Its aim was not only to control the mining in the state of Tennessee and to prevent chronic flooding in the area, but also to improve the living conditions of the local inhabitants
Sir Ernest Oppenheimer: a mine-owner and one of the richest men in South Africa (1880–1957)

Chapter 7

Jarvis pays a final visit to his son's house, and reads part of his son's autobiography.

NOTES AND GLOSSARY:
Negrophile: one who loves Negroes; in this context one who loves Negroes excessively
He cannot face it any more: the policeman feels that Jarvis had been overcome by grief. In fact he has learned new resolution, and that is why he need not come to the house again

Chapter 8

The Jarvises call on their niece and while James is reading Stephen Kumalo comes to deliver a message to a servant. Stephen is startled to find Jarvis there, but after a while he is able to confess that his son killed Arthur Jarvis. James reassures Stephen that he feels no anger.

NOTES AND GLOSSARY:
a man of the soil: more interested in farms and gardens than in conversation
which he did not do: even Jarvis cannot bring himself to have physical contact with a black African
I know you: Jarvis means no more than that he recognises Stephen as the parson from Ndotsheni. To Stephen, however, these words seem to identify him as the father of a murderer
unmanned: stripped of his manly reserve and control

Chapter 9

This chapter describes the strike of black mine-workers, and is built around a speech by John Kumalo and the reactions it inspires in other characters in the novel.

NOTES AND GLOSSARY:
the great bull voice: the voice of John Kumalo
Lansdown Commission: a Commission set up in 1943 to enquire into and report on the payment and working conditions of black workers in the Witwatersrand mines
Smit Commission: a Commission of 1942, which condemned the system of migrant labour
colour-bar: discrimination on the basis of colour
to go to prison would bring greatness: almost all of the political leaders of Central and West Africa spent time in prison
played with me: manipulated my emotions
grand stop of an organ: the control on an organ which makes it produce maximum volume
Yellow: cowardly
Annual Synod: this powerful body of clerics recommended in 1946 that the African Mine Workers' Union be recognised by the authorities. The recommendation was ignored. Thousands of members of the union went on strike in August 1946
a remarkably low loss of life: this chilling phrase expresses the callous indifference of many white employers to their black employees
deserted harbour: the harbour is deserted because of the absence of goods for export as a result of the strike
Behind the polished panelling: even in the expensive rooms which attempt to emulate European styles of architecture and furnishing, the reality of Africa is still felt

Chapter 10

Mrs Lithebe is increasingly worried about the behaviour of Gertrude, and warns her about her conduct. There is a report of another murder in the newspaper, and Msimangu and Mrs Lithebe conspire to keep the newspaper away from Stephen. After an evening church-meeting addressed by a nun, Gertrude announces that she would like to become a nun.

NOTES AND GLOSSARY:

I shall be glad to leave this place: Gertrude, one of the most fallible characters in the book, blames the place for her problems rather than admitting that the fault lies within her self

who worked for South Africa: who worked for the progress of the country as a whole rather than to pursue their own personal ambition

it is a hard thing: Msimangu is afraid that the judge will be influenced by the report of another murder, and will deal more harshly with Absalom

Chapter 11

Delivering his verdict, the judge finds that there is insufficient evidence to convict Absalom's friends and thus they are acquitted. Absalom, however, has confessed to the murder and the judge rules that there is no case for mercy. He is sentenced to death.

NOTES AND GLOSSARY:

lends colour to that supposition: makes the supposition appear more likely

our own complicity: the guilt that the whole society shares in the crime

to obtain: to be relevant

encompass: bring about

Chapter 12

In prison Absalom is married by Father Vincent. In a tense conversation with his father after the ceremony, Absalom talks of the arrangements he wants to make about his possessions and his family. Stephen goes to visit his brother John and, although Stephen tries hard to be charitable towards his brother, the two men quarrel and Stephen is thrown out of John's shop. Jarvis is preparing to leave for Ndotsheni, and gives John Harrison a donation of one thousand pounds for the boys' club, which he asks to be named in honour of his son.

Msimangu and Stephen say goodbye to one another, and Msimangu gives Stephen his Post Office savings book, containing over thirty pounds.

When Stephen wakes up on the morning of his departure he finds that Gertrude has disappeared.

NOTES AND GLOSSARY:

some great hope: Absalom hopes that they have brought news of a reprieve

I shall care for your child: these words are the first reference in the chapter to the fact that Absalom will not live to care for his child himself

they are not here now: Stephen's meaning is that the two boys are not under sentence of death. In fact, through an irony of circumstance, the two boys are in the prison and will stay there after Absalom has been transferred to Pretoria to be put to death

a great Judge: that is, God, who delivers the final judgement after death

the fatted calf will be killed here: an allusion to the parable of the prodigal son which John referred to in Book One, Chapter 14

I heard it: Stephen has not heard this at all. He invents the story in order to hurt his brother and to make him afraid

Helen of Troy: a mild oath expressive of John's surprise and excitement

gay party: happy occasion

a community: a religious order cut off from the world

the lie and the quarrel: the dispute with his brother John

BOOK THREE

Chapter 1

Stephen returns to Ndotsheni with the girl and the little boy. He is anxious at first about the questions that will be asked about his sister and his son, but he finds that his return is warmly welcomed by the people of the village. A friend tells him that the people know of Absalom's fate, and Stephen includes a reference to both his sister and his son in the prayers at the first service he gives after his return. After that service Stephen tells his friend about the misgivings he has about his ability to continue in Ndotsheni. His friend reassures him and Stephen returns home to his wife and his new family.

NOTES AND GLOSSARY:
battlefields of long ago: the Natal district of South Africa was the site of many battles between settlers and Zulus
talk like children: talk without restraint or embarrassment
it is nothing to ask: it is not considered ill-mannered to ask
It is known here: the people here know that Absalom shot Arthur Jarvis
she is cold with: she is unfriendly towards
They said also, they do not care: a reference back to Book Two, Chapter 8. James Jarvis had thought that Stephen had not heard this said

Chapter 2

Stephen is determined that something should be done to improve conditions in Ndotsheni. He visits the chief, and will not be put off by his promise to discuss the matter with the school inspector. He embarrasses the chief by pointing out that it is the poverty of the land which makes the children leave, not the school curriculum. The chief promises to see the magistrate and Stephen goes to visit the headmaster of the school. He finds little to cheer him at the school and returns to his church disheartened. Just then the grandson of James Jarvis rides by and shows a keen interest in the parson and his house. The boy asks for a drink of milk and is abashed to discover that there is no milk in the village. Stephen tells him that the children are dying in Ndotsheni because of this. That night a messenger arrives from the Jarvis farm with a cartload of milk and a promise that Jarvis will continue to supply milk until the drought comes to an end.

NOTES AND GLOSSARY:
knocked these chiefs down, and put them up again: the white settlers had gained control of the land by defeating the chiefs in battle, and then had attempted to keep control of the people by allowing the chiefs some token authority over their tribe
feeding an old man ... into a boy: paying lip-service to an outmoded system and pretending it would develop to serve the needs of the future
I have spoken ... before: the chief finds it difficult to admit that, despite his earlier meetings with the magistrate, there has been no improvement
perhaps not so academic: ironically the school garden presents a relevant lesson in that it contains only death
Jeepers creepers: a mild oath
respite: relief

small boys must bring water: in order to keep the milk cool
the day he says to me die, I shall die: the man wishes to convey the
extent of his respect for Jarvis

Chapter 3

Four letters arrive from Johannesburg. One, from the lawyer, explains
that there is to be no mercy for Absalom. Absalom's letter speaks
simply of the regret he feels for what he has done. As Stephen is
reading the third letter, from Msimangu, he notices the storm-clouds
gathering and is surprised to see a group of men arriving by motor car.
The party includes Jarvis, the magistrate and the chief, and they spend
some time placing sticks into the ground. Jarvis finds that he cannot
get back before the storm breaks and he takes shelter with Stephen in
the leaky church. After the storm has passed and Jarvis has gone, the
people of the village gather around the sticks, totally mystified as to
their purpose.

NOTES AND GLOSSARY:
nostalgia: a yearning for some past event or location
box on three legs: a surveyor's theodolite
babel of sound: mixture of voices
I do not understand...completely: I do not understand the legal
situation but I understand the grief you must feel

Chapter 4

Stephen continues to be visited by Jarvis's grandson. A young man
arrives in the village as an agricultural demonstrator, having been sent
for by Jarvis. He explains that the people must change their farming
methods completely if the land is to be saved. The Jarvis boy comes
back one last time before returning to Johannesburg.

NOTES AND GLOSSARY:
our medicines come mostly from trees: a great many drugs have a
natural source as their basis
our word is from your word: Zulu includes in its vocabulary a number
of words borrowed from English

Chapter 5

Stephen prepares to take a confirmation service when he hears news of
the death of Mrs Jarvis. Stephen does not feel that he can visit Jarvis,
but he sends a note expressing his sympathy. He is secretly afraid that
Mrs Jarvis may have died heartbroken at her son's murder. After the

confirmation service the bishop speaks to Stephen in private, and advises him that he should leave Ndotsheni, because he believes that living so close to Jarvis will prove intolerable. Stephen does not know how to tell him the truth, but a letter from Jarvis arrives at that moment and Stephen is thus able to reassure the bishop about his relationship with Jarvis. The people of the village make a wreath in memory of Mrs Jarvis.

NOTES AND GLOSSARY:

confirmation: the service in the Christian church in which ado-
                    lescents make a public affirmation of their com-
                    mitment to the church. This affirmation is made in
                    the presence of a bishop
Sunday clothes: best clothes
Comfort ye: a quotation from the Bible, Isaiah, 40
deem: judge

Chapter 6

The young demonstrator is able to make gradual changes in the farm-ing practices in Ndotsheni. There is little immediate progress because the goodwill of the people needs to be maintained. In conversation Stephen finds that the demonstrator has more radical political views than Stephen had suspected.

NOTES AND GLOSSARY:

the great machine: a bulldozer
another Napoleon: Napoleon Bonaparte (1769–1821), Emperor of
                      France from 1804
We would if we could: the demonstrator does not believe that it is
                      possible to work for South Africa: he must work
                      for the continent as a whole
I have a friend: an allusion to the corruption of his brother John

Chapter 7

Stephen goes up into the mountain on the night before his son's execu-tion, to pray and to contemplate. As he starts the climb he meets a man on horseback: it is James Jarvis. Jarvis tells Stephen that he is about to leave Ndotsheni, and Stephen thanks him for all he has done. Stephen spends the night thinking of his son, and also of the many kind people he has met during his life.

NOTES AND GLOSSARY:

the fourteenth day: Absalom is to be executed on the fifteenth day of
                      the month

near her time: about to have her baby
the hand that you eat with: the right hand
because this man was hungry: because this man was desperate to have
                        his opinions confirmed

Part 3

Commentary

History of publication

Cry, the Beloved Country was begun by Alan Paton in Trondheim, Norway in late September 1946. At that time Paton was in the middle of a tour of Europe and America, comparing their systems of penal reform with that in his native South Africa. He continued to write throughout his trip, completing his story in California. The typescript was submitted by friends of Paton to some fifteen publishers, nine of whom expressed interest. It did not take him long to decide to pursue the interest expressed by Maxwell Perkins, editor for Charles Scribner's who had published such famous American novelists as Scott Fitzgerald and Ernest Hemingway. The final manuscript was accepted on 7 February 1947 and the book was published in January 1948.*

The reception of the novel was phenomenal, not only because it opened the eyes of the world to the situation in South Africa, but also because of the intrinsic literary merits of the book. It was published in England almost simultaneously with its American publication, has since been translated into some twenty languages and has achieved a universal circulation.[†] The novel was filmed by Sir Alexander Korda in 1951, formed the basis of a musical tragedy by Maxwell Anderson and Kurt Weill in 1949, and was adapted as a verse drama by Felicia Komai in 1954.**

Sources

In the first volume of his autobiography Alan Paton comments that in 1946, during his trip to Sweden,

> I read for the first time John Steinbeck's *Grapes of Wrath*, and would soon adopt his style of rendering conversations, indicating by a preliminary dash that a speech was about to begin, and omitting all inverted commas. The novel made a deep impression on me.... Because of this it has been said that John Steinbeck has been an influence on my writing but in fact he was not (*Towards the Mountain*, p.269).

* See *Towards the Mountain*, p.297.
[†] See Callan, *Alan Paton*, p.22. ** ibid., p.139.

Despite this disclaimer there can be little doubt that there are substantial similarities between *The Grapes of Wrath** and *Cry, the Beloved Country* which go further than the mode of rendering conversation. Both novels attempt to expose an unjust social situation by integrating a fictional narrative and a set of real historical circumstances; both novels are based upon a journey, and in each case there is at one end of the journey a barren agricultural landscape and at the other the promise of a better future, which proves ultimately illusory; both novels make considerable use of imagery of birth and death; and *Cry, the Beloved Country* makes use of a narrative technique first employed by Steinbeck in *The Grapes of Wrath*: the introduction of inter-chapters. Steinbeck intersperses his main narrative, the story of the Joad family and their journey to California, with chapters of description of a more general kind. These chapters do not advance the narrative, and indeed do not include the Joads at all; but they provide the reader with a sense of the wider social context, and their inclusion makes the main narrative seem less a unique fictional event and more of an instance of a prevalent social phenomenon. Paton adopts this technique to a similar purpose in *Cry, the Beloved Country*, and such a chapter as Book One, Chapter 9, the description of conditions in Shanty Town, seems to owe a debt to Steinbeck. However, it will be argued below that Paton produces a much finer novel and employs the device of the inter-chapter with greater sophistication.

  Cry, the Beloved Country has a further source, one which it shares with *The Grapes of Wrath*. Both novels make considerable use of parables, situations, and language drawn from the Bible. *The Grapes of Wrath* takes its basic situation from the Old Testament book of Exodus as the Joads strive to reach in California their own Promised Land. It includes, also, a preacher whose initials are those of Jesus Christ and who, like Christ, lays down his life for the good of his people. Christianity and the Bible are more fundamental, however, to *Cry, the Beloved Country*, not only in the style and symbolism of the novel but in the whole spirit of the work.

Realism and parable

In his preface to the novel, Alan Paton alludes to its combination of realism and fiction: 'the story is not true, but considered as a social record it is the plain and simple truth.' Like Steinbeck, Paton is describing a situation which existed in reality but selecting a fictional narrative as the focus of this description. No novel can deal successfully with a social movement because the stuff of literature is

---

* John Steinbeck, *The Grapes of Wrath*, Viking Press, New York, 1939.

the focus upon an individual: its impact must come from the presentation of that individual in a way which we, the readers, can sympathise and identify with. Paton makes this clear in Chapter 10 of Book One through the outburst of Msimangu: 'I tell you, you can do nothing. Have you not troubles enough of your own? I tell you there are thousands such in Johannesburg.' There may be thousands like Absalom in Johannesburg, but Alan Paton seeks to engage our interest by concentrating upon the story of this one boy and his family, and the effect of the novel is increased rather than diminished by our knowledge that this story is not unique or untypical. Each of us will respond more readily and more passionately to a situation in which we have a personal involvement rather than to one in which we know only of the statistics, however large the numbers may be. Stephen Kumalo has a personal interest now in the question of 'native crime' because it is his son who is the criminal, and in a sense we, the readers, share that personal interest because we have, up to this point in the novel, perceived the situation through Stephen's eyes.

The novel describes a climate of political friction based upon conflicting ideologies, and these ideologies are graphically presented in the terms in which they are based, deriving in each case from a personal experience. Thus, for example, in Chapter 12 of Book One, we are presented with the viewpoint of one who believes that education will not cure delinquency, and we find that he holds that view because of his own experience: 'Let me give you a case. I had a boy working for me . . . . I treated him well and paid him well. Now do you know that . . . this self-same scoundrel . . . .' The novelist seeks to engage our interest as this speaker does, by describing events from a particular viewpoint. He must, however, also do what this speaker cannot do: he must demonstrate that this particular viewpoint is in some sense typical and that his argument is fair. Paton establishes the general truth of his story through a blend of realism and parable.

That the novel draws upon a real social context will be clear from Parts 1 and 2 of these Notes: the novel alludes to real people such as Professor Hoernlé and Sir Ernest Oppenheimer; it includes real events such as the bus boycott, the building of Shanty Town, the miners' strike, and the discovery of gold at Odendaalsrust; it describes vividly real locations such as Ixopo and Johannesburg. Some critics have sought to strengthen this evident realism by identifying fictional characters with real counterparts in South Africa's history,* but this seems scarcely necessary given a social context so obviously true.

Paton reinforces this kind of realism with another which manifests itself in his narrative method. He changes periodically from the past tense, typical of the narration in a novel, to a present tense which is

* See, for example, Callan, *Alan Paton*, p.53.

associated in the early part of the book with the inter-chapters of general description, but which gradually comes to be used also in the main narrative, where it helps to suggest that Absalom's story is not unique but typical of the fate of boys of his race and generation. This is particularly effective in the chapters describing Absalom's trial, where the use of the present tense lifts the narrative from a regionalist, documentary account and makes it seem that a larger trial is being enacted, the perpetual trial of a tribe. Similarly, when Stephen Kumalo first learns of Arthur Jarvis's murder, Paton moves us quickly from this individual instance to the general issue, partly through a shift to the present tense and partly through the inclusion of a lyricism based upon the language of the Bible and of the Psalms in particular:

> Sadness and fear and hate, how they well up in the heart and mind, whenever one opens the pages of these messengers of doom [newspapers]. Cry for the broken tribe, for the law and the custom that is gone. Aye, and cry aloud for the man who is dead, for the woman and children bereaved. Cry, the beloved country, these things are not yet at an end (*Book 1, Chapter 11*).

In this case the move from the individual to the tribe and then to the country as a whole is a simple and smooth transition, for the fates of all three coincide. One of the great strengths of the novel, however, is its presentation of situations in which national and personal issues are not in harmony but in conflict. A good instance of such a situation occurs in Chapter 8 of Book One where Stephen's personal desire to pursue his search for his son comes into conflict with the need of all black South Africans to boycott the buses. Thus in this instance the fictional narrative of Stephen Kumalo meets head-on with the real national politics of South Africa, and the national interests have to be given precedence. A similar conflict, this time couched entirely within the fictional framework, occurs in Chapter 2 of Book Two where Harrison recounts how Arthur Jarvis put his political convictions before his personal interests in speaking against the compound system.

Paton also establishes the general truth of his narrative by a skilful use of parable, which counterbalances the realism of the setting. A parable is a simple fable told to illustrate a moral, and it is a mainstay of the teaching of Christianity, since Jesus himself used parables as a means of instruction. In a very general sense the novel as a whole could be interpreted as a parable which conveys a message about the nature of brotherhood. Stephen is let down and, ultimately, disowned by his natural brother, but finds instead support and love coming from a man who is not even of his own race. However, there are other senses in which parable is significant within the novel: some are related to its overall Christian ethos, others to its theme of education.

Stephen Kumalo, as an Anglican minister, tends naturally to use parables and to see his own life in terms of parables, and Alan Paton makes extensive use of this natural tendency. Thus, when he is swindled by the young man at the Johannesburg bus station, Stephen relates this to his earlier boastfulness in the train, and he reflects upon this on his arrival at the Mission House: 'Kumalo could not boast any more . . . . He spoke humbly. I am much confused, he said. I owe much to our friend' (*Book 1, Chapter 4*).

Stephen's son is called Absalom, and this name should alert us to the possible outcome of his quest, for Absalom was the favoured son of David who rebelled against his father David and who occasioned the lament of his father upon his death (see the Bible, II Samuel, 18). Stephen's brother John twice refers to the parable of the prodigal son, the son whose dissolute life was nevertheless forgiven by his loving father: it is a mark of John Kumalo's lack of vision that he cannot see that there are situations in which love alone is not enough to bring a happy ending. Thus, although the novel may make these allusions to parables, it avoids presenting the reader with neat, simplistic solutions. All does not end happily in the novel because the book does not absolve its characters from personal responsibility for their actions. There may be occasions which appear to be divine intervention (such as the timely arrival of the letter from Jarvis in Chapter 5 of Book Three), but the outcome of events ultimately stems from human action.

Parables are essentially part of a mechanism of education and they are used as such in *Cry, the Beloved Country*. The novel is concerned with the education of several of its characters, and also with the education of the readers. Absalom, before the novel begins, has already been educated into the corruption of the city, but the novel concentrates more extensively on the education necessary for Stephen Kumalo and for James Jarvis. Stephen uses a parable in conversation with Father Vincent to describe his incomprehension of his situation:

> There is a man sleeping in the grass, said Kumalo. And over him is gathering the greatest storm of all his days. Such lightning and thunder will come there as have never been seen before, bringing death and destruction. People hurry home past him, to places safe from danger. And whether they do not see him there in the grass, or whether they fear to halt even a moment, they do not wake him, they let him be (*Book 1, Chapter 15*).

It is for the unnamed friend in Book Three to explain to Stephen what the parson cannot see for himself: that his education has been to learn the meaning of suffering itself:

> I have never thought that a Christian would be free of suffering, umfundisi. For our Lord suffered. And I come to believe that He

suffered, not to save us from suffering, but to teach us how to bear suffering (*Book 3, Chapter 1*).

James Jarvis, too, is educated in the course of the novel, as he comes to appreciate the political standpoint of his son: a viewpoint he hardly knew existed before his son's death. Although some of this education comes through conversations with John Harrison, the most impressive educational medium is the written word of Arthur Jarvis himself. Thus *Cry, the Beloved Country* is in a sense a book about writing, and about the effects that writing can have in educating the reader. Ideally we, as readers of the novel, should be educated at the same time as the characters within the book. As Edward Callan writes:

> What it does objectify is individual recognition of personal responsibility. Such recognition depends on a process of self-discovery, a process which both James Jarvis and Stephen Kumalo endure in the novel . . . . Ideally, the reader of *Cry, the Beloved Country* undergoes a process of self-discovery, too (*Alan Paton*, p.66).

Quest and journey

The principal source of dynamism in the novel is provided through the quests undertaken by the central characters. Any literary narrative must provide a challenge for its main protagonist and the challenge in *Cry, the Beloved Country* is the quest of Stephen Kumalo to find his family and to rebuild the tribe. We, the readers, follow this quest and participate in it: in a lesser novel the structure of the book would be entirely determined by this quest and the work would end with its successful completion. We are familiar with this kind of pattern from fairy-tales and romances in which parents and children are separated for a while only to be happily reunited at the end. Alan Paton knows that we have this at the back of our minds and deliberately frustrates that expectation in order to demonstrate to us and to Stephen Kumalo that the rebuilding of the tribe is not a simple exercise. Stephen's quest continues after his journey has ended, and can only be brought to a successful conclusion when he is back home again.

The ideas of 'quest', 'journey', 'search', and 'pilgrimage' intersect throughout the novel and we may notice that Stephen, having arrived in Johannesburg, thinks to himself: 'In good time no doubt they would come to discuss the reason for his pilgrimage safely at an end (*Book 1, Chapter 4*). In fact, in this novel which is full of beginnings and endings, the pilgrimage is only just starting. Just as a Christian pilgrim visits the locations associated with one who has led an exemplary life, so Stephen, in his search for Absalom, visits the places where his son has been and thus relives the journey of Absalom's life in the city. The

metaphor of life as a journey, a prevalent metaphor in Christian literature, underlies much of the novel, for Stephen is clearly presented as
one who is not only a stranger in the city but also a child in its ways. His
journey in Johannesburg moves from the ingenuousness of a child, as
he is described on his arrival (*Book 1, Chapter 4*)—'The room was
light, and the great bewildering town shut out. He puffed like a child at
his smoke, and was thankful.'—and passes through a process of education to a mature understanding of the complexity of the South African
situation. In this, Father Vincent is able to convey to him the
significant lesson that 'Fear is a journey, a terrible journey, but sorrow
is at least an arriving' (*Book 1, Chapter 15*).

Stephen makes two significant journeys in the course of the novel:
the first from Ndotsheni to the city, which he undertakes with a proud
self-importance; the second back to Ndotsheni again, full of humility
and shame. These changes of location help Stephen to establish a sense
of perspective about the place he has left and to reflect productively
upon the meaning of his experiences. A similar function is served by
the brief respite in Chapter 13 of Book One when Stephen temporarily
adjourns his quest in order to visit Ezenzeleni with Msimangu. From
the perspective of Ezenzeleni Stephen can see more clearly what he has
learned from Johannesburg, just as from the city he could see what
needed to be done in Ndotsheni.

This use of perspectives in the novel corresponds to the circumstances of Alan Paton's own life, for he too moved from Ixopo to
Johannesburg, and, moreover, he found that he could write most
lucidly about South Africa when he was physically distanced from it,
from the perspective provided by his tour abroad.

The structure of the novel

The novel is composed in three books, which Edward Callan has
described as follows: 'Book One . . . might be described as the Book of
Kumalo . . . . Book Two is the Book of James Jarvis . . . . Book Three is
the Book of Restoration' (*Alan Paton*, p.62–3). Although we might
wish to extend and amplify these descriptions, they provide a useful
basis for discussion of the structure of the work. Certainly Book Two
provides a fresh start within the novel: we retrace our steps over events
we have already seen taking place within Book One, but this time from
the viewpoint of James Jarvis rather than that of Stephen Kumalo.
Thus, just as the novel provides us with a range of locational perspectives, each of which illuminates the other, so its structure provides contrasting ideological perspectives which ultimately reinforce one another.

In order for this reinforcement to be effective Paton must make
Kumalo and Jarvis similar to each other and yet keep them essentially

different. Thus, although both men come from the same area, although each has a son who has gone to the city and is leading a life which his father does not understand, although each loses his son, and even though each journeys to Johannesburg to find him (Stephen in a physical sense, James in a spiritual sense), they are nevertheless very different from each other, and the Johannesburgs which they find are different too, for one man is black whilst the other is white. This difference is made very clear at two points in Book Two: one in Chapter 8 when the two men meet, by accident; the other in Chapter 12 as each takes his separate leave of the city. At the time of their meeting there is no doubt that the two men are not socially equal: it is Jarvis who has the superior status, a status which has nothing to do with the murder of Arthur Jarvis. However sympathetic Jarvis may feel to Stephen, he cannot bring himself to touch him: 'such a thing is not so lightly done as picking up a stick'. At the time of their departure from Johannesburg the two men have very different experiences. Stephen, whose departure is described in greater detail, quarrels with his brother, loses his sister, and receives with gratitude Msimangu's gift of thirty-three pounds: his total wordly wealth. In contrast, James Jarvis gives rather than receives, and is able to donate one thousand pounds for the boys' club which is to be a memorial to his son.

Book One and Book Two are set in contrast with one another and both are different in kind from Book Three. The first two books not only introduce the individual perspectives of Stephen Kumalo and James Jarvis, they also present different racial perspectives, for whilst Book One is largely concerned with the tensions between black and white, Book Two introduces the tensions within the white race between Afrikaners and English-speaking South Africans. This tension is presented largely through the viewpoint of Harrison, who, in Chapter 2 of Book Two, disapproves of Arthur Jarvis's having learned Afrikaans; but it is manifest also in the inter-chapters of the second book. However, the two opening books are not kept artificially discrete, each dealing neatly with its separate area, for the suspicion of the Afrikaners felt by the English-speaking whites is alluded to twice within the first book: once in Chapter 12 where the views of the two European churches are contrasted:

> The English-speaking churches cry for more education, and more opportunity, and for a removal of the restrictions on native labour and enterprise. And the Afrikaans-speaking churches want to see the native people given opportunity to develop along their own lines . . . .*

---

* The novel is not, of course, uncritical of the English-speaking South Africans, as the characterisation of Harrison makes clear.

and again in Chapter 13 where Stephen notices with surprise that in Ezenzeleni

> It was white men who did this work of mercy, and some of them spoke English and some spoke Afrikaans. Yes, those who spoke English and those who spoke Afrikaans came together to open the eyes of black men that were blind.

The resolution for this particular issue comes not in Book Three as we might expect but in Chapter 4 of Book Two, where the funeral of Arthur Jarvis is described. It is attended by people of all races, and thus Arthur Jarvis in death becomes the resolution for much of the racial conflict in the novel.

Book Three is described by Edward Callan as the 'Book of Restoration'. It is also, unlike the earlier two books, the book of Ndotsheni. Each of the other two books starts with the same lyrical description of Ixopo, but each moves rapidly to the city where the beauty of the hills is forgotten, except in the reminiscences of Stephen Kumalo. Book Three stays in Ixopo and in an Ixopo where Kumalo and Jarvis no longer remain isolated from one another, each in his separate world. The lyricism of description is this time continued throughout the book, and is combined with a symbolism drawn from nature. This symbolism was hinted at in the opening of Book Two, as James Jarvis gazed at the sky and searched anxiously for a rain-cloud. It is fully developed in the final book where the rain, when it comes, not only brings back the life blood to the land but also exposes the holes in the church roof; it brings about the meeting between Jarvis and Kumaldo as James shelters from the storm, and almost disrupts the confirmation service. Nature can be cruel or kind, and man must learn to accept both its faces.

Beginnings and endings

It was pointed out above that Stephen Kumalo believes that his pilgrimage is at an end when he reaches the Mission House in Sophiatown, whereas in fact it is only just beginning. The novel is full of such beginnings which arise out of apparent endings: they are appropriate to the sub-title which Alan Paton gave to his work, 'A Story of Comfort in Desolation'. Both Stephen Kumalo and James Jarvis experience such comfort arising from desolation, and this is part of the balancing of the two characters which occurs throughout the novel. One manifestation of this juxtaposition of beginnings and endings comes through the balancing of adults and children and of death and birth in the novel.

Both Stephen and James lose their sons during the course of the novel, and although the circumstances of the two deaths are dissimilar,

each is in a sense the death of a child in Africa and might be seen as a
desolate and hopeless event. However, each man also has a grandchild,
and the death of a son is in each case juxtaposed with the birth of a new
life. In the case of Stephen Kumalo this juxtaposition is achieved quite
straightforwardly: his daughter-in-law is about to go into labour on the
very night when his son awaits execution. In the case of James Jarvis
the juxtaposition is effected more subtly in that we are introduced to
Arthur Jarvis's children only at the moment when we learn of his
murder; thus, although his son has been alive before the murder, in a
literary sense he is born into the novel at his father's death.

Children are powerful and evocative symbols in that they represent a
hope for the future, which may or may not be realised. Stephen himself
displays the innocence of a child in his bewilderment in Johannesburg,
when, for example, he suggests to his brother John that they telephone
Absalom's employer to ask for his whereabouts. However, such frank-
ness and innocence can be extremely productive elsewhere in the novel:
when Jarvis's grandson asks for milk his naiveté leads to the provision
of milk for the village children. Without his enquiry nothing would
have happened. Kumalo is touched and comforted by the unaffected
joy which the children of Ndotsheni show on his return to the village,
and his principal hope for the future lies in the grandchild which is
being carried by his new daughter, herself merely a child.

However, the novel as a whole must leave the reader questioning
whether Stephen's hope for the future is likely to be realised. Absalom,
the boy who was to have gone to St Chad's, is hanged in a Pretoria
prison; and Arthur Jarvis, once a 'small bright boy', is murdered by
accident in Johannesburg. The novel tells us quite clearly that to be a
child of South Africa is no easy thing for black or white. In Book One
the unborn child is a symbol of hope, but an inheritor of fear:

> Cry, the beloved country, for the unborn child that is the inheritor
> of our fear. Let him not love the earth too deeply .... For fear will
> rob him of all if he gives too much (*Book 1, Chapter 12*).

and in Book Two the brief autobiographical sketch by Arthur Jarvis
presents the difficulties from a white standpoint:

> I was born on a farm, brought up by honourable parents, given all
> that a child, could need or desire .... From them I learned all that a
> child should learn of honour and charity and generosity. But of
> South Africa I learned nothing at all (*Book 2, Chapter 7*).

Thus, one of the messages of this novel written some thirty-five years
ago is that hope cannot come from an inheritance of fear, and that fear
cannot be dispelled while people live in ignorance of their compatriots.
Yet the ignorance and the fear persist. Donald Woods, in a recent

biography of the black leader Stephen Biko, describes his own upbring-
ing as a white South African in the following terms:

> My early view of blacks was therefore of backward people, few of
> whom could read or write, most of whom wore loin-cloths and blan-
> kets, not 'European clothes', and people in the grip of extreme
> superstition . . . one of whose effects appeared to be an alarming
> degree of callousness and cruelty (*Biko*, p.37).

It is illuminating to set this account of a South African childhood
against this dialogue between an Afrikaner and the novelist Doris
Lessing on the subject of racial inequality:

> 'But they're nothing but children, man! You must know that. Look
> how they live! It makes me just about sick to go into one of their
> locations. Besides, I don't like their colour, I just don't like it.' He
> paused, very serious, wrestling with himself. 'You think I've just
> been brought up to be like that?'*

Variety in language and character

One of the most impressive features of *Cry, the Beloved Country* is the
range of voices which it includes. Paton is attempting to reflect the
various tones which go to make up the voices of South Africa,† from
its many races and diverse ideologies. We may feel now that the novel is
too diverse and attempts to describe a complex situation from too
many different viewpoints for a single novel to contain. However,
given the date of its composition and the likely audience of the novel, it
is scarcely surprising that Alan Paton should have chosen to expose a
broadly based situation rather than to focus upon a single issue within
it.

Technically the novel is a *tour de force*, a composite of different
styles, ranging from the brusqueness of Harrison to the formality of
the exchange between Stephen and the child at the opening of the
novel, from simple narrative to descriptive lyricism to the biting satire
of such a passage as this from Book One, Chapter 12: 'Oh, it's too hot
to argue. Get your racquet, my dear, they're calling us . . . . You've got
to play like a demon, do you hear?' Something of this range of styles is
exemplified in the Specimen Answer in Part 4 of these Notes, and in
this section we shall concentrate upon the function of this range.

Although the novel is written entirely in English it is attempting to
convey the complexities of a situation in which within one country
many different languages are spoken, all by people who have a valid

---

* Doris Lessing, *Going Home*, Panther, St Albans, 1968, p.24.
† See Callan, *Alan Paton*, Chapter 3.

claim to call themselves South Africans. People can be linked by a common language or divided by their inability to communicate, and Alan Paton is careful to indicate the extent to which language determines relationships. Thus, when Stephen Kumalo comes to Johannesburg he finds that a rift has developed between himself and the family he seeks, and that this rift is reflected linguistically in three different ways. When he meets his sister Gertrude, the first member of his family he re-discovers, he finds that her very voice has changed:

> She calls, but the voice that was once so sweet has a new quality in it, the quality of the laughter that he heard in the house. She is revealing herself to him (*Book 1, Chapter 6*).

Gertrude is revealing herself to her brother through the quality of her voice, and also to us as readers, for we have the sweet quality of the rural voice already in the voice of the narrator and in Stephen's description of his home; so we too mourn its absence in Gertrude.

When Stephen finds his brother John it is not the voice which has altered (although the voice of John Kumalo is a significant force in the novel as we shall see below), but the very language which he speaks:

> —But I do not understand. How is life different in Johannesburg?
> —Well, that is difficult. Do you mind if I speak in English? I can explain these things better in English (*Book 1, Chapter 7*).

The things that John can only explain in English cannot in fact be explained at all, for they lie at the roots of the corrupt and immoral life he is leading in the city. Once again language divides the family when it should unite it.

Stephen's separation from his son is also reinforced by a linguistic divide, this time the most terrible of all, when two men speak and no meaning at all is conveyed:

> —I have searched in every place for you.
> To that also no answer. The old man loosens his hands, and his son's hand slips from them lifelessly. There is a barrier here, a wall, something that cuts off one from the other (*Book 1, Chapter 14*).

As one kind of communication is broken down within the family in Book One, so another is established outside it in Book Two. Arthur Jarvis was, like Alan Paton himself, multilingual, and one of the delights in the relationship between his son and Stephen Kumalo is that the little boy wants to learn Zulu. In the final chapter there is a moving conversation between the novel's two principal characters, Kumalo and Jarvis, and although it is not clear in what language they are speaking, what is evident is that their language has dignity, and can effect real communication:

> Because Jarvis made no answer he sought for words to explain it,
> but before he had spoken a word, the other had already spoken.
> I understand you, he said, I understand completely (*Book 3,
> Chapter 7*).

The words 'I understand you completely' have been used earlier in the
novel by characters sympathetic to the needs of others, and here, in the
mouth of James Jarvis they are, at the conclusion of the book, a fitting
testimony to his new-found sensitivity.

There is one further sense in which the novel emphasises the power
of language, and that is in the weight it places on the two contrasting
voices of the novel's most mighty orators: John Kumalo and the
Reverend Msimangu. Here we have the contrast between the world of
politics and the spiritual world of religion, as Paton presents us with
John's speech about the strike in Book Two, Chapter 9 and invites us
to compare it with Msimangu's sermon at Ezenzeleni in Book One,
Chapter 13. There can be no doubt that we are intended to be more
impressed by the sermon, and to be dissatisfied by the political voice.
John Kumalo lacks full commitment, speaks from self-interest, and
for one purpose only: to hear the applause of the crowd. Whereas
Msimangu not only speaks out of disinterest but even denies that he has
any responsibility for the beneficial effects of his sermon:

> he talks humbly, there is no pride or false constraint.
> —I have tried every way to touch you, he says, but I could not
> come near. So give thanks and be satisfied (*Book 1, Chapter 13*).

There is a variety of character in the novel to correspond with its
linguistic range. We are introduced to characters from a number of
different races and age-groups, and this sweep of humanity is further
extended in the inter-chapters so that we feel that the whole country has
participated in the book.

Much has been said in the preceding pages about the characters of
the two principal protagonists and it is perhaps more useful at this
point to make some general observations about Alan Paton's method
of characterisation. Notice, firstly, that he does not idealise his
characters, for none of them are made to seem perfect. His central
character, Stephen Kumalo, has the flaws of humanity but he is able at
the end of the novel to face up to his sins, and to list them for himself
(and for us):

> There were some he remembered easily, the lie in the train, the lie to
> his brother, when John had barred the door against him and shut
> him out in the street; his loss of faith in Johannesburg, and his desire
> to hurt the girl, the sinning and innocent child. All this he did as fully
> as he could, and prayed for absolution (*Book 3, Chapter 7*).

The only case where the novelist appears in danger of idealisation is in his presentation of Arthur Jarvis, for it is difficult not to idealise those who die young, with promise yet unfulfilled. However, even here there is a possible reason for his method, in that Arthur Jarvis influences other characters in the novel primarily through the inspiration he provides in his writings and not as a conventional character might. It is fitting, therefore, that he should be presented in the manner which Alan Paton chooses.

We may feel that some of the characters in the novel are insufficiently drawn to justify their inclusion: the novel has almost thirty characters, some of whom are never named, even though they may play a substantial part in the narrative. We may wonder why, for example, the friend to whom Stephen confides in Book Three is not identified, or why the daughter-in-law remains always as 'the girl'. We might also question the way in which some of the named characters, especially the women, are dealt with. Stephen's wife (again unnamed) seems to have a major function in the opening pages of the novel in emphasising her husband's stubbornness, but this function is not developed. Similarly, Margaret Jarvis seems to function more as someone to be looked after by her husband and, eventually, lost by him than as a character in her own right; and, although we know that James Jarvis has a granddaughter, it is only the grandson who features in the narrative. Indeed it seems that in the novel as a whole the attitude to women is like that of Absalom Kumalo contemplating the birth of his child:

—If the child is a son, I should like his name to be Peter ...
—And if it is a daughter.
—No, if it is a daughter, I have not thought of any name (*Book 2, Chapter 12*).

However, merely by listing the characters who appear in the novel, one of its principal tensions is revealed: this is a book about two families, the Kumalos and the Jarvises, who interact not only as families but against a context of South African society with its judges, chiefs, agricultural demonstrators, bishops and priests. All of these functionaries have an interest in the fates of Absalom and Arthur, but only for their families can that interest ever become personal and unique. As Stephen points out to Father Vincent:

... others saw it. It was revealed to others to whom it did not matter. They saw it, step by step. They said, this is Johannesburg, this is a boy going wrong, as other boys have gone wrong in Johannesburg. But to us, for whom it was life and death, it was not revealed (*Book 1, Chapter 14*).

Evaluating the novel

Perhaps the fairest method of evaluating the success of *Cry, the Beloved Country* is to set the novel alongside, on the one hand, the novel closest to it in intention and, on the other, the other major novel by Alan Paton. John Steinbeck's *The Grapes of Wrath* provides one point of perspective, *Too Late the Phalarope* the other.

The Grapes of Wrath was written with a similar purpose to that of *Cry, the Beloved Country*, in that it sought to investigate a particular case of social injustice and to expose that case through the medium of fiction. However, *The Grapes of Wrath* is a far less satisfactory novel because it is too obviously based on research work, written out of a comparatively slender acquaintance with the people and the issues being described. It has been criticised for factual inaccuracies of a geographical, linguistic, and botanical kind: it is inconceivable that *Cry, the Beloved Country* could contain such flaws because the book is written from the point of view not of one who has spent a month or two investigating a particular issue but rather by a writer who has lived through the problem from birth. The problems described are also different: the South African problem is more complex, less easy to solve; it was more in need of exposure to an international audience. It may seem now, with the benefit of hindsight, that the plight of the Okies described by Steinbeck was, in comparison to the situation described in *Cry, the Beloved Country*, a transitory and regional phenomenon. Both works, however, bring us back to the fundamental question raised by William Empson in a classic piece of literary criticism written over thirty years ago: can literature written about the working classes really be politically significant when its readership is not proletarian but middle-class?*

Cry, the Beloved Country, nevertheless, contains an ingredient entirely absent from *The Grapes of Wrath*. Steinbeck's novel is angry without providing any source for resolution: its Okies are entirely right, its Californian vineyard-owners entirely wrong, and there is no faith in the power of humility to effect a solution. Alan Paton has written instead a great Christian novel in which, although characters may be racially either black and white, they are morally more complex, and which expresses a fundamental optimism in humanity and its ability to effect change.

The lyricism which is the single most impressive feature of the novel is a lyricism born of Christianity, in which the pilgrimage of a life through suffering still retains hope of a better goal:

* William Empson, *Some Versions of Pastoral*, Chatto & Windus, London, 1935. See particularly Chapter 1, 'Proletarian literature'.

Who knows for what we live, and struggle and die? Who knows what keeps us living and struggling, while all things break about us? ...this, the purpose of our lives, the end of all our struggle, is beyond all human wisdom (*Book 1, Chapter 10*).

It is the Bible which sustains Stephen Kumalo throughout the novel, from the trauma of the train journey to the wretchedness of his home-coming to Ndotsheni. This is his 'comfort in desolation', the source of true brotherhood which can outweigh the false brotherhood of John Kumalo, and the force which can combine politics and family, and can transcend them both:

Call, O small boy, with the long and tremulous cry that echoes over the hills. Dance, O small boy, with the first slow steps of the dance that is for yourself. Call and dance, Innocence, call and dance while you may. For this is a prelude, it is only a beginning (*Book 3, Chapter 1*).

Too Late the Phalarope is not, like its predecessor, a sustained invocation or prayer for general harmony. It is written for a different purpose, and one which is more evidently literary. It does not vary the pace of its narrative to include the general comments of inter-chapters, nor does it attempt either the multiplicity of voice nor the emotional impact of the earlier novel. It is, in a sense, a better novel, in that it is more conventionally novelistic. Its focus is tighter on an issue which is more sharply defined, and thus it is able to investigate its smaller range of characters in greater depth. For all of these reasons it is a most rewarding novel which requires a greater concentration from the reader than *Cry, the Beloved Country*. It demonstrates that Alan Paton is not only the master of the documentary style of novel, but can also write a sustained work of fiction which evokes very powerfully the pressure of one single issue within South African life.

Part 4

Hints for study

Studying a novel

Most students of *Cry, the Beloved Country* will be preparing to answer essay questions for examinations. Questions on the book will define quite precisely what aspect is to be written about (there are some sample essay topics included in this text): it is clearly impossible for any student to write all that he knows of the novel in a single essay. However, you should not be afraid to challenge the question given to you: it may well be deliberately couched in the form of a quotation about the text which is only partially true, and may invite you to state what the limitations are of that particular approach to the novel.

The reader of novels or plays is initially interested in the characters of the participants. Indeed the success of the work may well rest in the reader's ability to understand why a particular character behaves in the way that he does: to sympathise with the character.

To write a study of a character in *Cry, the Beloved Country* you need to establish the following points:

(1) List the situations in which the character appears.
(2) Note what is said by the character.
(3) Note what is said to the character.
(4) Note what is said about the character (either by the narrator or by other characters in the book).
(5) Note what is said about the character in those incidents in which the character does not appear.
(6) Note the way in which the character might change or develop in the course of the novel.

Not all the characters in the novel are made equally significant, and you need to bear this in mind in tackling an essay question. Stephen Kumalo is obviously the central character, the one most involved in the narrative and the most subject to change in the course of the novel. It is unlikely that an essay question would require a full character study of Stephen: the subject is simply too large. Questions on this character will probably ask for an investigation of his behaviour with reference to one particular incident. However, it is quite possible that a question on a lesser character such as Father Vincent would require a full discussion of the role which he plays throughout the book.

It is easy to forget that Alan Paton chooses to tell the story from one particular viewpoint and that the material is not sacrosanct. It is a useful exercise to attempt to put yourself in the position of the writer and to reconstruct the kinds of choices he had to make. For example, we might consider how different the novel might be if it began from the perspective of James Jarvis, and if Stephen Kumalo were not introduced until the beginning of Book Two. Or we might experiment by imagining the whole narrative from the viewpoint of one of the minor characters: Harrison, for example, or the young man at the reformatory. Any one of these exercises will be helpful in investigating the mechanism of the novel itself, and in engaging with its writing. More radical experiments would include attempting to edit the novel by, for example, dispensing with the descriptive inter-chapters, or by omitting certain of the characters. Radical editing of this kind can often shed light on the composition of the original text, and can reveal why all its facets are, indeed, essential.

Whilst working on the investigation of the novel it is by no means essential to do so independently: indeed in the case of a book like *Cry, the Beloved Country* which has been successfully adapted for the stage it should be particularly helpful to work on the text with others by reading it aloud. You might also try opening up discussion in groups by each selecting what for you is the key sentence (or even the key word) in a chapter, and then justifying your selection to the rest of the group.

In writing about *Cry, the Beloved Country* you are performing the task of a literary critic, and in carrying out that role you must ensure that you adhere to a key critical principle: that your writing does not do a disservice to the text. You must avoid making the novel seem in your essays to be less rich or less complex than it is in reality. Thus it is necessary to avoid statements which schematise the book into a series of equations. This is a trap which it is especially easy to fall into when writing about characters, and you need to beware of describing characters as if they represent some single quality throughout the book. In a novel as good as *Cry, the Beloved Country* the characters, especially the principal characters, undergo a process of education and will therefore develop and change in the course of the work. You will do the best service to the novel if your essays indicate, wherever it is appropriate, the developments and dynamism within the book.

Sample essay questions

(1) Illustrate the ways in which the novel can be said to be concerned with beginnings and endings.

(2) What does the device of the narrative inter-chapters contribute to the novel?

(3) Compare and contrast the presentation and the function in the novel of Mrs Kumalo and Margaret Jarvis.

(4) Demonstrate the ways in which the introduction of James Jarvis relies upon our acquaintance with Stephen Kumalo.

(5) What is the significance of Stephen's visit to Ezenzeleni?

(6) How does the novel benefit from the range of locations it includes?

(7) How successfully does the novel combine elements of parable and of realism?

(8) How essential to the novel is its Christian setting?

(9) What are the benefits, and the restrictions, of the novel's three-book structure?

(10) Illustrate the variety of language and style in the novel.

Specimen answer

In order to demonstrate the way in which a particular essay question might be approached, there follows a specimen answer to question (10) above. After this essay you will find an explanation of why it takes the form it does.

---

(10) Illustrate the variety of language and style in the novel.

Alan Paton includes variation in language in two different respects in *Cry, the Beloved Country*: he varies his style according to the race of the characters involved, and he also varies it to suit the situation of different incidents.

The two races principally involved in the novel are the Zulu and English-speaking South African, and within each group there is a spectrum of styles. The first conversational exchange in the novel, for example, establishes the dignity and formality of Zulu in the dialogue between Stephen Kumalo and the small girl who brings his letter. Some of this formality is reflected also in the non-spoken language of the inter-chapters. For example, in the description of the construction of Shanty Town, we find the repetition of a question which becomes almost a refrain: 'Have you a room that you could let?'

Not all the instances of Zulu-based languages are formal, however, for Alan Paton also includes some examples of black South Africans struggling to master English, as, for example, in the letter which James Jarvis finds in his son's study, a letter which combines technical errors with an obvious sincerity.

The principal Zulu voice in the novel is, of course, that of Stephen Kumalo, and Alan Paton makes it clear that Stephen's own style owes a good deal to the language of the Bible. Thus, for example, when Stephen is locked out of his brother's shop at the end of Book Two, the style of the narrative takes on the tone of a biblical narrative:

> And none of these things had he done. God have mercy on me, Christ have mercy on me. He turned the door, but it was locked and bolted. Brother had shut out brother, from the same womb had they come.

Stephen's own power as a narrator also derives from that simplicity which is generally associated with the Bible, as, for example, in his description of his homeland early in Book One:

> He told them too of the sickness of the land, and how the grass had disappeared, and of the dongas that ran from hill to valley, and valley to hill; . . . how the tribe was broken, and the house broken, and the man broken; how when they went away, many never came back, many never wrote any more.

This passage includes a further quality of language which is prevalent in the novel. In introducing the words 'the tribe was broken' Alan Paton is providing a link between this and other passages in the novel, for this is a recurrent line, one of a number of repeated lines which are spread across the novel. Other examples are the comment 'such a thing is not lightly done', and the spoken line 'I understand you completely.'

The variety of style within the English-speaking characters in the novel ranges from the sensitive and personalised writing of Arthur Jarvis to the brusque speech of Harrison with its rather out-dated English slang. Within the inter-chapters, too, there is variation of voices, including the anti-Afrikaner voice who speaks of the discovery of gold at Odendaalsrust and the conflicting European voices who debate the question of 'native crime'.

This debate is one example of the way in which Alan Paton varies language to suit different situations. The debate is couched in the appropriate formal style, with its repeated addresses to 'Mr Chairman' and its resolutions. Yet, even within this same chapter other styles are present, including the informal chat of the white women at the Tennis Club. The novel encompasses a whole range of situations, each of which demands a different style. Thus, for example, we move from the language of Christian worship, in the service at Ezenzeleni, to that of the court, in the trial of Absalom Kumalo. There is a similar range, too, in written communication, which includes the various letters from Msimangu, Stephen Kumalo and James Jarvis, the newspaper reports of Arthur's murder, and the essays of Arthur Jarvis himself.

Thus we see that the novel includes a full range of styles, appropriate to the variety of people and of situations presented in the book.

This essay was written from a simple plan which firstly established the major divisions within the essay, and then listed examples of the kinds of variation which were to be included. The essay has an introduction which briefly sets out the approach to be adopted and thus gives the reader an idea of the scope of the work. The introduction predicts that variation will be demonstrated in terms of race and situation, and each of the examples which is included in the bulk of the essay is related to one or other of these two major divisions. It is more profitable to include one example from each sub-division, rather than to have many examples of the same phenomenon (for example, of formal Zulu conversational exchanges): the interest of the reader is more easily sustained through this variation, and the breadth of the novel more effectively illustrated. It is not necessary to quote word for word from the novel on every occasion (although the specimen answer does include some quotations); what is necessary is a precise reference to the context which will enable the reader to identify the passage or incident under discussion and will also convince him of your detailed knowledge of the novel.

Part 5

Suggestions for further reading

The text

PATON, ALAN: *Cry, the Beloved Country*, Charles Scribner's Sons, New York, 1948; Jonathan Cape, London, 1948; Penguin Books, Harmondsworth, 1958.

Other works by Alan Paton

Alan Paton has written a large number of articles on the political situation in his country. The list below includes only works of fiction and such political writing as is generally available in lending libraries.

Too Late the Phalarope, Jonathan Cape, London, 1953.

Debbie Go Home, Jonathan Cape, London, 1961. A collection of short stories, many of them based on experiences of reformatory life.

Hofmeyr, Oxford University Press, London, 1964. A biography.

Apartheid and the Archbishop: the Life and Times of Geoffrey Clayton, Archbishop of Capetown, Jonathan Cape, London, 1973. A biography.

Towards the Mountain, Scribners, New York, 1980. The first volume of autobiography (up to 1948).

Ah, But Your Land is Beautiful, Jonathan Cape, London, 1981.

Criticism

Although there have been numerous articles written on Alan Paton, especially at the time of the publication of *Cry, the Beloved Country*, few of these are now generally available and there has been no substantial single study of his fiction.

CALLAN, E.: *Alan Paton*, Twayne, New York, 1968. A biography (up to 1968) with an interesting analysis of Paton's fiction up to that date together with a substantial bibliography of his writings.

DAVIES, H.: *A Mirror for the Ministry in Modern Novels*, Oxford University Press, London, 1960. Includes a chapter on *Cry, the Beloved Country*.

PARKER, K. (ED.): *The South African Novel in English*, Macmillan, London, 1978. Includes comment on Paton.

PRESCOTT, O.: *In My Opinion*, Bobbs-Merrill, New York, 1952. Includes *Cry, the Beloved Country* as one of the four great novels of recent years.

Background reading

It would clearly be possible to compile a lengthy list of texts which provide useful perspectives on Alan Paton's novels. The list below is selective and includes texts which have been particularly useful in the writing of these Notes. The reader might profitably supplement this list with novels by such authors as C.J. Driver, Dan Jacobson, Doris Lessing and Tom Sharpe.

ACHEBE, C.: *No Longer at Ease*, Heinemann, London, 1960. A novel describing the corruption of the city in West Africa.

BANTON, M.: *Race Relations*, Tavistock, London, 1967. A description of race relations examined internationally.

MARQUARD, L.: *The Peoples and Policies of South Africa*, Oxford University Press, London, 1960. Written by a leader of the Liberal Party.

MULLARD, C.: *Black Britain*, Allen & Unwin, London, 1973. The first autobiography of a British-born black.

NEAME, L.E.: *The History of Apartheid*, Pall Mall, London, 1962.

SEGAL, R.: *The Race War*, Penguin Books, Harmondsworth, 1967.

SELBY, J.: *A Short History of South Africa*, Allen & Unwin, London, 1973.

STEINBECK, J.: *The Grapes of Wrath*, Viking Press, New York, 1939. One of the principal sources for *Cry, the Beloved Country*.

WALKER, ERIC A.: *A History of Southern Africa*, Longman, London, 1962.

WOODS, D.: *Biko*, Paddington Press, London, 1978.

The author of these notes

GEOFFREY RIDDEN was educated at the West Hartlepool Grammar School for Boys and at the University of Leeds before taking up a lectureship at the University of Ghana. He subsequently held posts at the University of Durham, at Westfield College, London, and at University College, London. He is currently Principal Lecturer in English at King Alfred's College, Winchester and Course Director of the B.A. English programmes. He has published a number of articles and reviews, and is the author of York Notes on *The Taming of the Shrew*, *Shakespeare's Sonnets*, *The Lord of the Rings*, and *The Hobbit*. He is also the author of the forthcoming York Handbook *Studying Milton*.